"Larry's vast knowledge of guitar playing is awesome.
His harmonic concepts and improvisational genius
have always established Larry as a true master!
This book should open the door to a better understanding
in our quest for advanced guitar playing."—*Al DiMeola*

"I recall a 1960s jam session in Seattle where,
for at least three hours in a quiet spot away from the main session,
a talented kid with his guitar hung out with an older gentleman and his guitar.
The kid was Larry Coryell; the older gentleman
was the jazz guitar master, Wes Montgomery.
Now years later, you have the opportunity to hang out with
and learn from the jazz guitar master, Larry Coryell.
What a trip!"—*Jerome Gray*

"As a professional musician, scholar and jazz educator,
I consider Larry Coryell's jazz guitar book
one of the most comprehensive text books available to the young jazz musician.
This book is not only great for guitar players,
but it helps saxophone players and other instrumentalists
understand the role of the guitar
in comping, soloing and improvising."—*Nathan Davis, Ph.D.,*
Director of Jazz Studies, University of Pittsburgh

"An easy to understand text
from one of the 20th century's greatest improvisors."—*Vic Juris*

Dedication

This book is dedicated to
John LaChapelle, my first guitar teacher
Jerome Gray, my first jazz teacher

To my mentor in life, Daisaku Ikeda,
who taught me the real value of education

ACKNOWLEDGMENTS

Greg Hofmann, for helping to shape the text
Jesse Gress, for his high standards in music notation

The Larry Coryell signature model guitar, LCS-1 by Cort,
was used to record the instructional CD.

LaRRy CoRyeLL
JaZZ GUiTaR

CREATIVE COMPING, SOLOING, AND IMPROV

MF Miller Freeman Books

San Francisco

Published by Miller Freeman Books
600 Harrison Street, San Francisco, CA 94107
Publishers of *Keyboard, Bass Player,* and *Guitar Player* magazines

 Miller Freeman
A United News & Media publication

Distributed to the book trade in the U.S. and Canada by
Publishers Group West, 1700 Fourth Street, Berkeley, CA 94710

Distributed to the music trade in the U.S. and Canada by Hal Leonard
Publishing, P.O. Box 13819, Milwaukee, WI 53213

Design and Typesetting: Greene Design
Editor: Greg Hofmann
Music Editor: Jesse Gress
Music Typesetting: Chris Ledgerwood
Cover Photo: Larry is pictured on the front cover with the
Larry Coryell signature model, LCS-1 by Cort.

Coryell, Larry.
    Jazz guitar : creative comping, soloing, and improv / by Larry Coryell.
        p.   cm.
    ISBN 0-87930-550-9
    1. Guitar—Methods (Jazz)   2. Jazz—Instruction and study.
I. Title.
MT582.C695   1998
787.87'165'143—dc21   98-41679
                                                       CIP
                                                       MN

Printed in the United States of America
    00 01 02 03   5 4 3 2

C O N T E N T S

Introduction
. . . vi

CHAPTER ONE
Jazz Basics: The Blues
. . . 9

CHAPTER TWO
Integrating Chords and Scales into
Jazz Language
. . . 23

CHAPTER THREE
More Scales and Fingerings
. . . 35

CHAPTER FOUR
Elements of Improv
. . . 53

CHAPTER FIVE
Playing and Listening
. . . 75

About the Author
. . . 94

What's on the CD
. . . 96

INTRODUCTION

If you're a guitarist who wants to improve your ability to play over changes, better understand jazz harmony, and expand your jazz vocabulary, this book is for you. My intention is to show you how I developed my own learning process over the years, and to point out what's important in order to get more inside the changes, to get inside the process of creating an improvised line and the thinking that goes along with developing skills in specific areas.

For instance, everyone knows and loves the blues, but jazz blues can be approached many ways, and there can be several kinds of changes, plus substitutes for those changes. And there's the whole area of improv—knowing and making up phrases that serve a particular role, and knowing how to be flexible within certain rules in order to avoid too many clichés that don't take the music forward. We'll walk the fine line between respecting cliches in order to sound authentic and breaking out of more predictable ideas to create a modernity in the music, to be "forward-sounding."

I want to teach—as much as is possible to teach—about the *feeling* involved in this music, and I hope that the playing on the CD will help; sometimes, if you can hear what's on the printed page, you're better able to understand it. If you want to learn how to comp alone, and within a group context, as well as learn how to solo in single lines and in chords, I expect you to *work*.

We begin by plunging directly into realistic jazz subjects, advancing step by step and working only with ideas and techniques that I think are essential to the creative process. There are many wonderful methods of learning guitar, but let's shelve the nonessential areas for other times and other books.

You should have a working knowledge of theory, at least some theory (that's all I have), and I'll assume you know some jazz chords and the fundamental major, minor, augmented (whole tone) and diminished scales and arpeggios. If you're less than solid in some of these areas, don't worry—I'll explain these elements as we go along. The material covered here is sometimes easy, but some of it gets involved and there are some examples/exercises I hope will challenge you and open you up to play things maybe you didn't think you could play. That's how I felt when I first heard jazz players make this amazing music on their guitars—I had no idea how it was done, but I *had* to try to learn it. If this rings a bell with you, let's go and make some music.

Photo: Anna Grossman

Photo: Bob Malik

CHAPTER ONE

Jazz Basics: The Blues

I think it's important to be able to play accompaniment (or "comp") with chords and bass-line phrases before you try your hand at soloing. Let's start with some chords and bass lines over a standard twelve-bar blues progression. There are many possibilities, but Example 1.1 is a middle-of-the-road set of changes that will give you something to work with. This chord progression uses the idea of playing two chords per measure.

Ex. 1.1

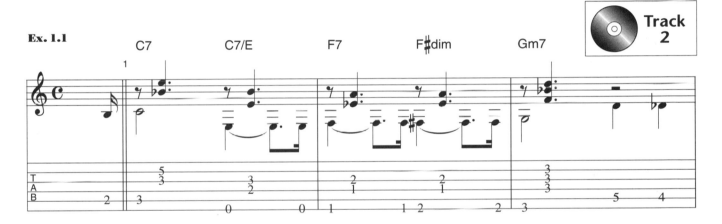

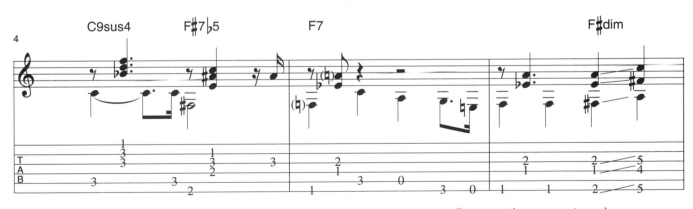

(lesson continues on next page)

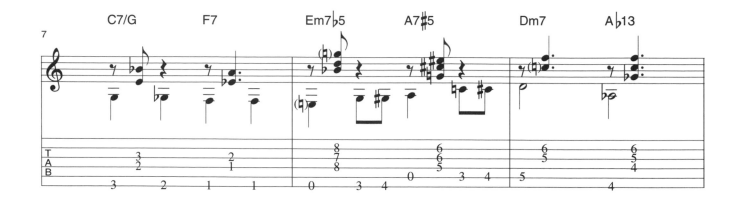

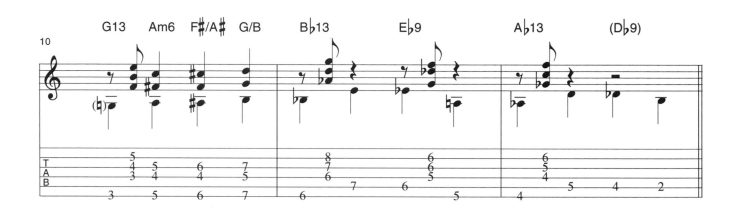

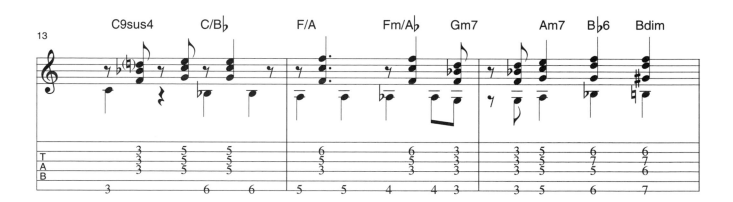

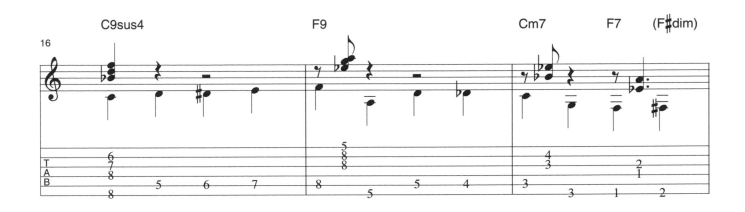

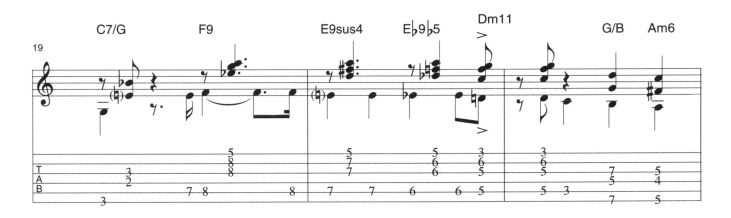

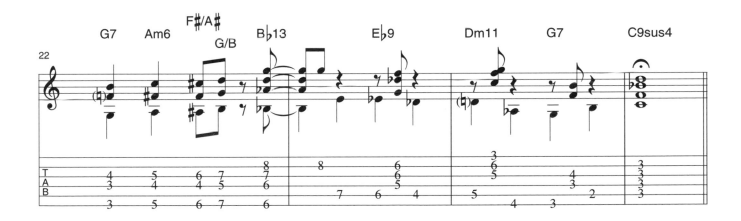

Let's look at the bass line. In the first three bars, we have a walking bass line that should sound familiar, going from C down to E then moving up in half-steps to G. We want to use recognizable phrases from the vast pool of jazz and blues vocabulary to ensure that it sounds "jazzy." The bass lines in Example 1.1 are meant to create, in tandem with the syncopated upper structure of two- and three-note chords, a moving "carpet" of rhythm and harmony.

We can also track chord movement using Roman numerals to name the chords as they function within the key signature, and Arabic numerals to show intervals within chords or between melody notes. Starting with C as I, we can spell out the progression as I7 for 2 beats, I7/3 for 2 beats, IV7 for two beats, #IVdim7 for 2 beats, and so on. Example 1.2 shows the progression of Example 1.1 using this system. The Arabic numeral under the Roman numeral names the interval used as the bass note; in other words, in bar 10 the #IV/3 means an F# major chord (the #IV chord) over an A# bass note (the 3 of F#). I suggest you learn this naming system because it helps when you transpose progressions to other keys or when you need to tell another player, "Play a II-V-I in A♭," or "Take that III-VI-II-V/3 progression up a whole-step."

Ex. 1.2

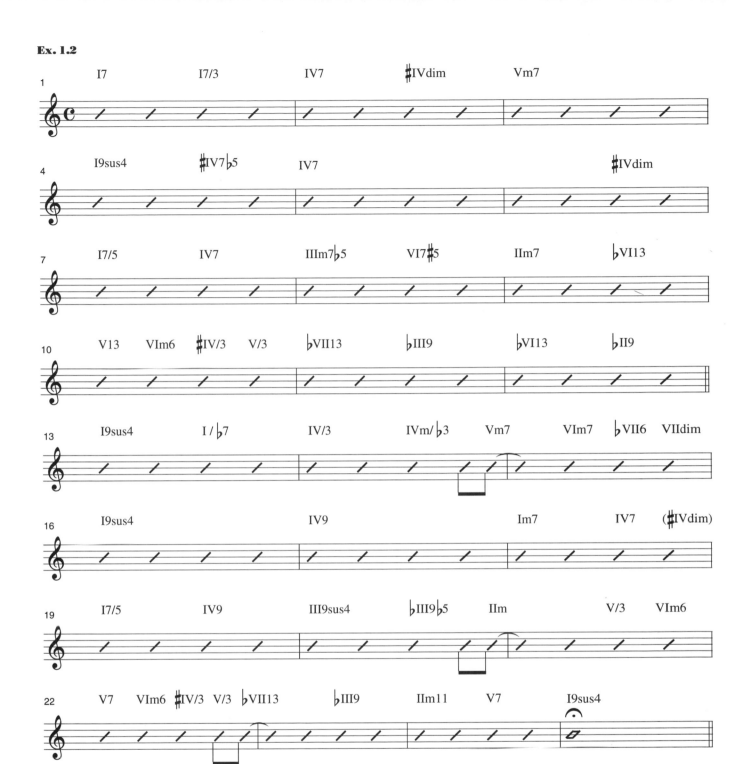

A word about the "9sus4" chord. Don't confuse this with a chord spelled 1-4-5, bottom to top, which is technically a suspended 4th chord with no 3rd. What is meant here is 1-♭7-9-11 (as in the first chord of bar 4 in Example 1.1) or 1-4-♭7-9 (as in the first chord of bar 13—the same voicing comes again in bar 16 and the same voicing, this time in E, is in bar 20).

Now listen to Example 1.4, which combines the comping thing we did in Example 1.1 with solo passages. This is a sample of how to shift from the comp mode into solo mode and back. First, here are the scales that are used for the single lines; when improvising, one needs to know the scales for the chords, and, more importantly, how they are used:

Ex. 1.3a

F Mixolydian

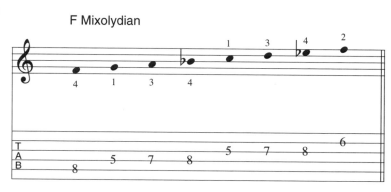

D Dorian with C♯ leading tone

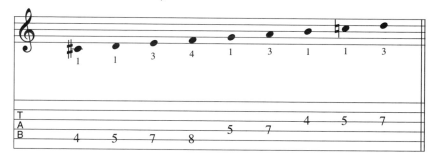

C Pentatonic minor

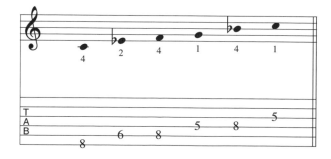

C Mixolydian

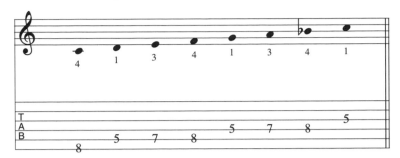

Half-whole diminished starting from B

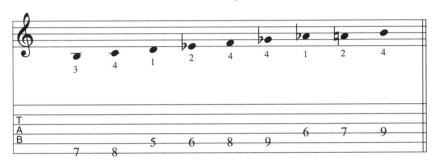

D harmonic minor starting from A

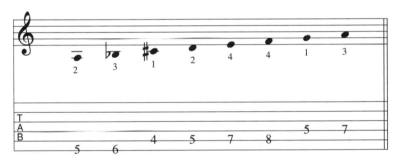

I'll show you some more scales in Example 2.1, but now let's look
at the full comp-and-single-line example:

Ex. 1.4

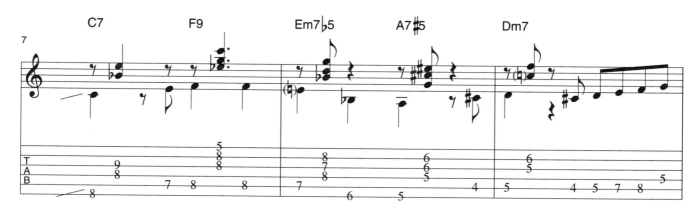

The first solo phrase (in bars 2–4) draws from F Mixolydian; just after that, the four notes in the extra first half of bar 4, E-G-D-C, come from C Mixolydian. When I got to bar 9, I played a C# leading tone into a Dorian ascending scale, which is connected to the C Ionian mode, or CMaj, scale. There are many improv occasions where we will use the scale as the basis for an idea. For example, I threw in some chromatic notes (leading tones) between the mode notes to lead up to that C in bar 11. I used the half-whole diminished starting from B for bars 17 and 18 to cover the F7(IV7) going into the F#(#IV) diminished. In the 20th bar, I used part of a D harmonic minor scale with A as the tonal center—that covered the VI chord. I soloed through the turnaround (the last two bars of 12-bar form) of the first chorus with C pentatonic and C Mixo. We'll look at another way to solo through a turnaround when we get to the end of the first chorus of Example 2.2.

Example 1.5 mixes comping with solo passages, but this time the passages are chords in the upper register. There are times when the left hand should stay put, but many more occasions (like this one) where we need to move around the neck quickly. The chord-solo passages are played with traditional big-band phrasing.

Track 4

Ex. 1.5

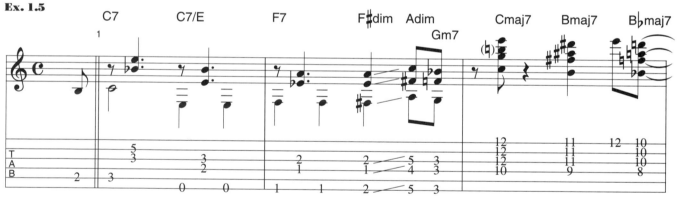

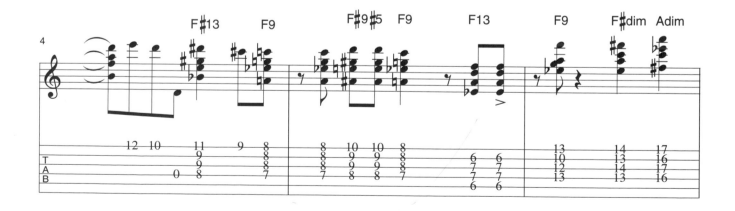

(lesson continues on next page)

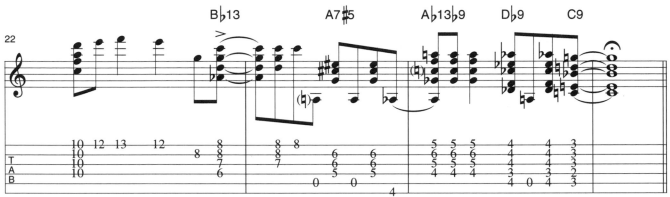

In the first chorus, all the solo-voiced chords are on strings one through four. There is minor-third sliding (like the F♯dim7 to Adim7 in bar 6) and different voicings for essentially the same chord (Dm7 in bars 9–11). In the second chorus, there are more minor-third slides with diminished chords (played on strings two through five in bar 16) and again, the first four voicings in bars 21–22 are essentially Dm7. I try to be faithful to big-band phrasing by inserting a few single notes in the chord-solo passages, as in bar 17; take away the harmony notes, and you have the single line shown in Example 1.6.

Ex. 1.6

There's a similar example of this four and one-half bars later:

Ex. 1.7

Add the harmony to these single lines and you get a big-band sound.

We've looked at some blues ideas and variations to give us points of reference. Comping and soloing are two sides of the same coin. One supports and depends on the other and, in a sense, soloing is responding to comping by creating good phrasing. Of course, the comping has to be good in order for the soloist to do his or her best work. We will go deeper into comping in Chapter 5. At this juncture, however, there are more elements of the blues I want to show. First, let's look more closely at the scales that relate best to the chords we've been playing, and also at some chord-scales.

Photo: Ken Franckling

CHAPTER TWO

Integrating Chords and Scales into Jazz Language

When I first started playing, I transcribed solos from records—Barney Kessel, Tal Farlow, Kenny Burrell, Johnny Smith, and especially Wes Montgomery. I didn't have any jazz vocabulary at the time, and I didn't have any idea of the subtle elements that make up a good solo. So, first by learning and then by analyzing the musical thinking of these accomplished players, I began to see how improvisations were constructed. I would transcribe one of Wes's pieces, and then I'd see, "Aha, here he's playing a substitution for the tonic," or "That augmented arpeggio works well on the altered chord." It was hard work, but it paid off.

In this chapter, I'll take you through some musical analysis in detail, working with the blues we started learning in Chapter 1—both single-line and chord work—and then getting into an area beyond the blues.

First, have a look at the scales in Example 2.1.

Ex. 2.1

"Charged-up" C Mixo-Pentatonic ♭5

"Charged-up" F Mixo ♭5

(lesson continues on next page)

Ex. 2.1

A Super-Locrian

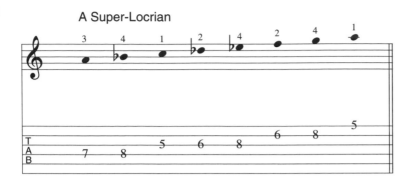

G Mixolydian

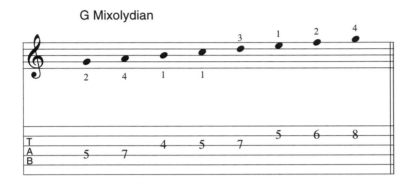

F Dorian

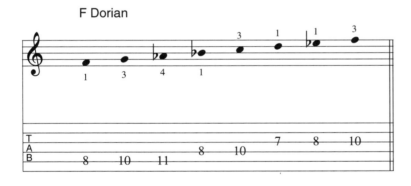

B♭ Dorian

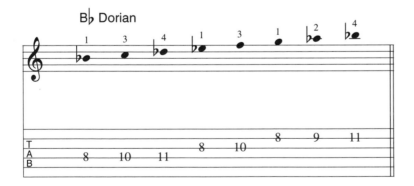

E♭ Dorian

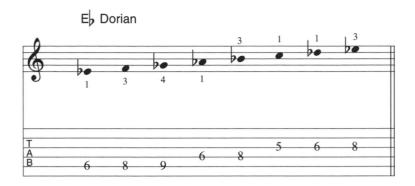

A♭ Dorian ♯4

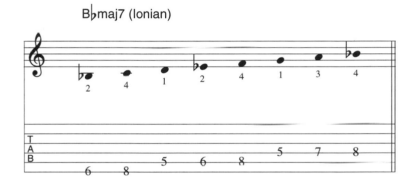

B♭maj7 (Ionian)

Gmaj7 (Ionian)

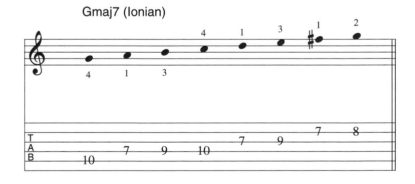

These scales are similar to those introduced in Example 1.3. However, I "charged up" the C Mixo, which is now chromatic between the ♭3 and the 5, and the F Mixo, which now has a fragment of the half-whole diminished starting from B. A C pentatonic fits inside both scales; I renamed them "charged-up" C Mixo and "charged-up" F Mixo. They can also be defined as C Mixo-pentatonic-♭5 and F Mixo-♭5.

There's now an A Superlocrian scale for playing VI7 chords; if you start this scale from B♭ you have the parent mode, B♭ jazz minor. Example 2.2, which is a solo over the "basic track" of Example 1.1, shows all the scales in Example 2.1 at work.

Ex. 2.2

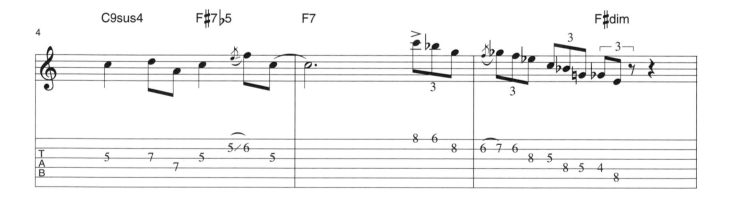

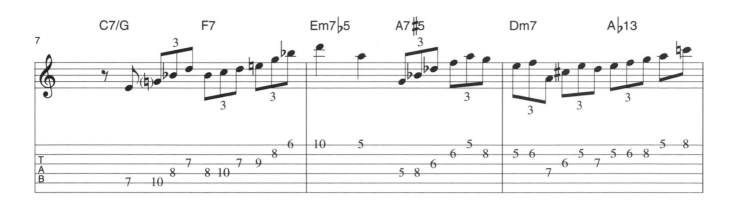

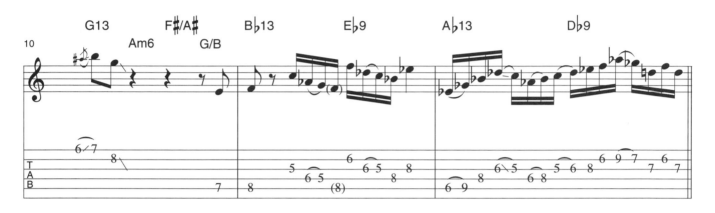

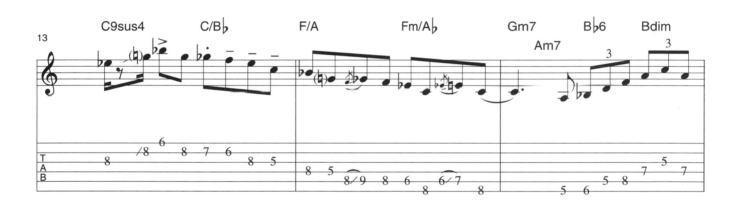

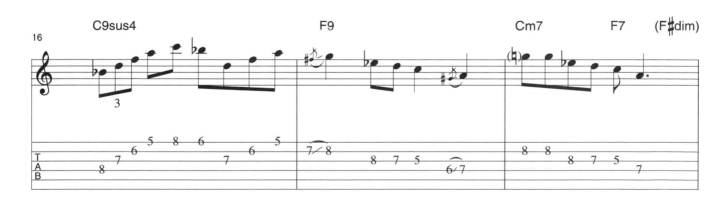

(lesson continues on next page)

Integrating Chords and Scales into Jazz Language

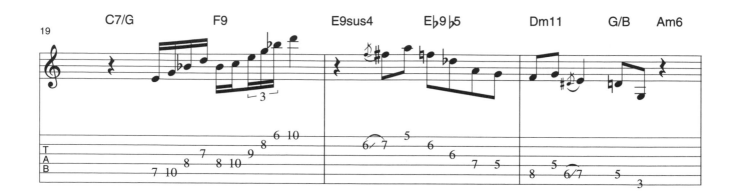

In bar 7, we used a straight C Mixo, arpeggiating a C9 into the Em7♭5 in the first half of bar 8. For the second half of bar 8, I arpeggiated the A Superlocrian mode. Only a part of the G Mixo is used in bar 10 and in bar 24. For the first turnaround (bars 11–12), I drew from the four Dorian scales to play the B♭13-E♭9-A♭13-D♭9, with each scale starting from the fifth degree of the chord root. The B♭ major scale (Ionian mode) is a substitute for a simple C Mixo in bars 15–16 and the G major (only two notes are used) fits in the E9sus4, bar 20.

In the 2nd chorus turnaround, the blue notes (B♭, G♭, and E♭) in the C Mixo-pentatonic-♭5 work in ♭VII7 (B♭13) and ♭III7 (E♭9) as well as the IIm7 (Dm11) in bar 24; a blues phrase with an E♭ works here even though the Dm11 is straight diatonic.

OK, we've looked at how to apply some single-note scales to the jazz language. Now let's work with chord-scales. Example 2.3 gets us started with something easy: a chord-scale in C diatonic tonality—just the white notes on the piano. Play it as written, ascending, and take it back down the same way.

Track 9

Ex. 2.3

C Diatonic chord-scale

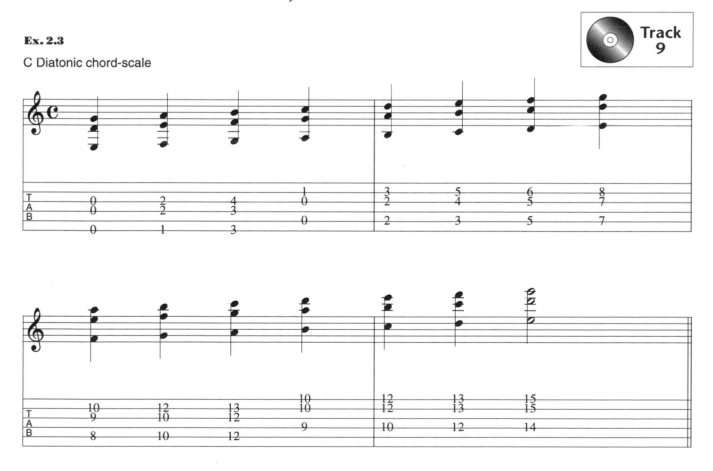

Example 2.4a shows a C Mixo chord-scale that goes up using one set of voicings and descends with different voicings. Example 2.4b gives you six substitute voicings for the first three bars to show some of the options in situations like this.

Ex. 2.4a

C Mixolydian chord-scale

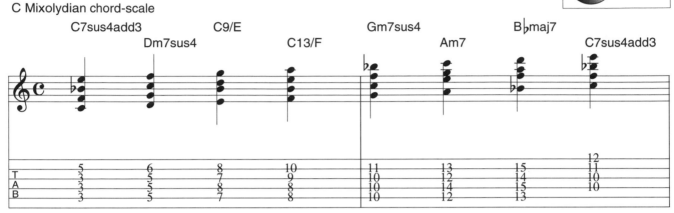

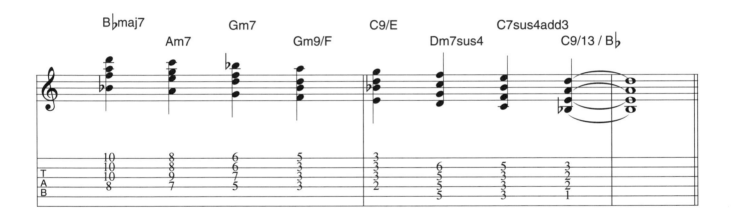

C Mixolydian chord-scale w/substitute voicings

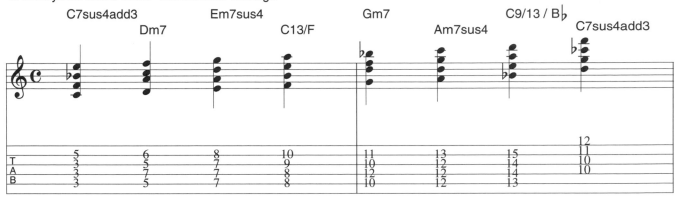

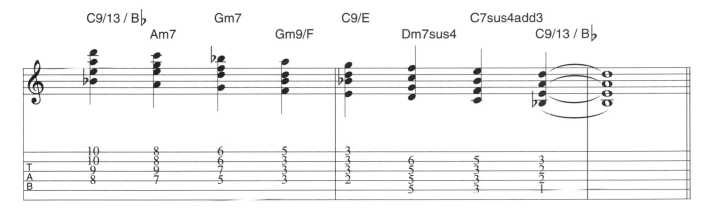

You should know about alternate voicings within a chord-scale because you want to be able to go outside the Mixo mode.

For example, in the fourth chord in the 2.4a sequence you might want to play an F7sus4 (with an E♭ on the third string rather than the E natural that's there now).

Let's work more with this idea of alternate voicings within a chord-scale. Example 2.5 is a C Dorian chord-scale:

Ex. 2.5

C Dorian chord-scale

A couple of comments: Using the bottom note of each chord as the guide-note, the scale goes up one full octave plus another three steps, stopping on F. Also, all the m7 chords are actually m7sus4s. The 3rd degree chord in the second octave, E♭maj7, is different than its counterpart in the first: F13 (which has no F in it—the root is assumed). Now that we have the C Dorian chord-scale, we can divide an F7 into related voicings. Let's see what we can do with it—maybe take it out of a strict blues context without losing the blues essence. Example 2.6 shows one way.

Track 13

Ex. 2.6

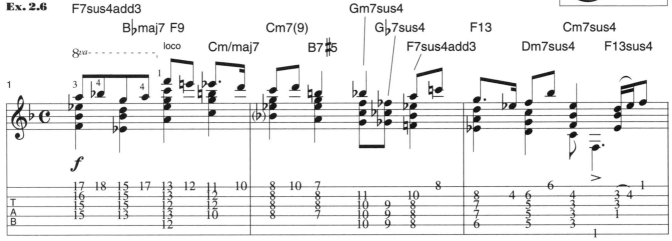

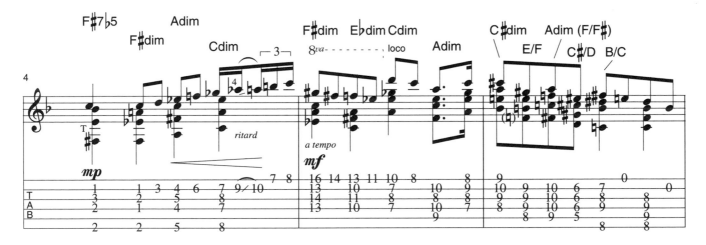

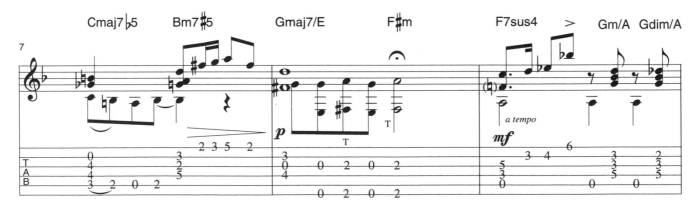

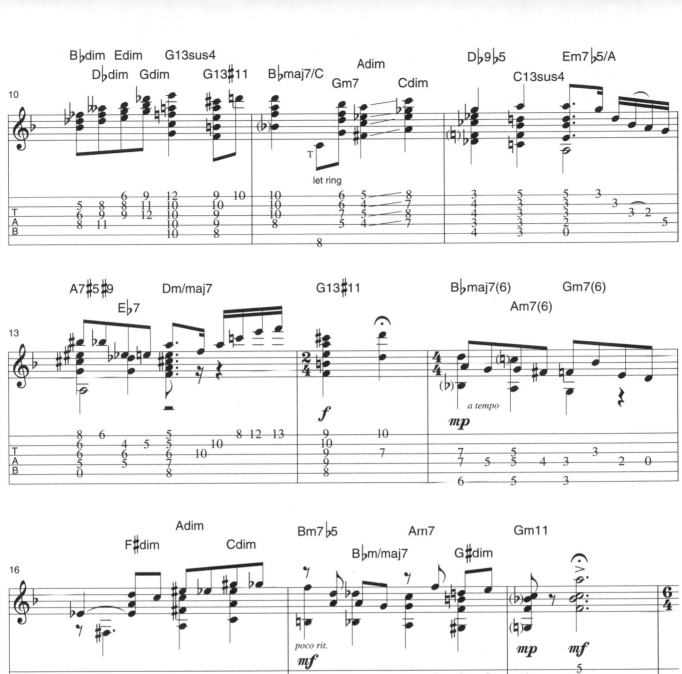

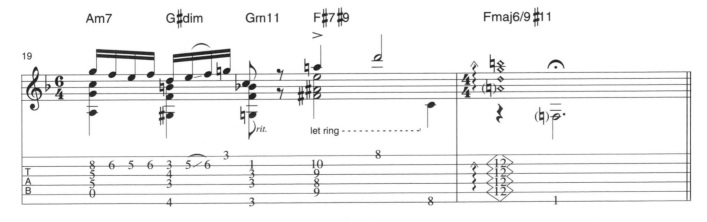

In bars 1–3, the thinking process goes like this: Start by splitting the F7 into Cm7-F7, then extend those chords into E♭maj7, F9, Cm/maj7, Cm7, F9♯11, and so on. With the Cm/maj7 and F9♯11, we go briefly into the C jazz minor mode, C Dorian's neighbor. The example also goes out of the mode for an instant in the 2nd bar, 3rd beat with the descending Gm7 to G♭m7 (out of the mode right there) to the F7sus4 (back in).

Now look at bar 4. This is our half-whole diminished scale dressed up in chords, only the sequence begins with whole-half—C to D to E♭ to F to G♭, and so on. The single notes, 4th beat, bar 4 lead to a descending chord passage in the same diminished scale. The diminished chord tonality goes up a half step, 1st chord, bar 6, then returns to the half-whole starting from B tonality with the 2nd chord. The Bmaj/C, 2nd half of bar 6, is another chord that fits in that "half-whole starting from B" tonality. In bar 7 of Example 2.6, the voicing of the first chord, Cmaj7♭5, is similar to the Bmaj/C chords in bar 6. Now, by dropping the C down a half step to B, the tonality becomes E minor.

More Scales and Fingerings

When I was touring with saxophonist Benny Golson a few years ago, we were looking for some new tunes to play, so I wrote out a minor blues called "Turkish Coffee" and took it up to his room. I was amazed at the way he played through the changes using scales and arpeggios, choosing the most meaningful intervals to define the chords. For some reason, I thought that he would just gloss over the progression and play some blues-by-ear to the chords, but the way he dug into the harmony in detail brought me back to the reality of who I was working with—a true jazz giant whose proximity to other tenor players like Coltrane and Jimmy Heath (the Philadelphia school) helped form his own prodigious concept of improv.

So let's dig deeper into these chords, get inside some of the changes, and try to extract some *music* from them, the way Benny Golson did. Example 3.1 shows a standard minor blues progression.

Ex. 3.1

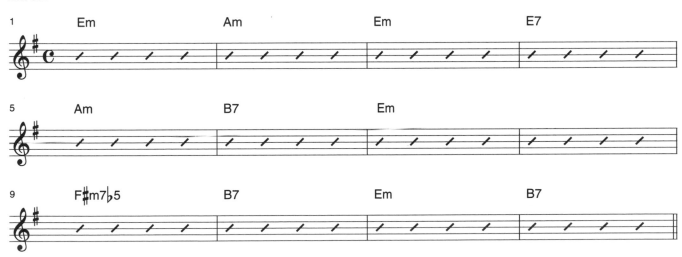

Now let's look at "Turkish Coffee," a minor blues, with a chord for every beat (except the last half-measure).

Ex. 3.2

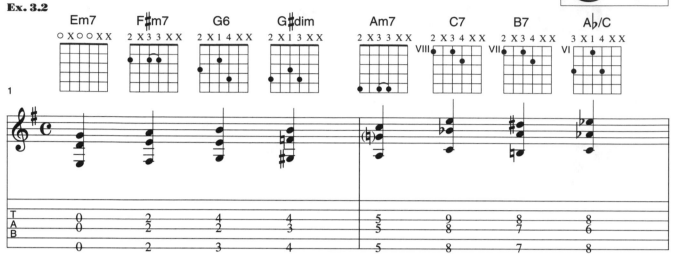

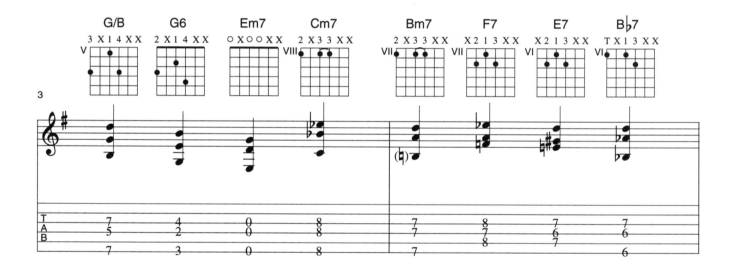

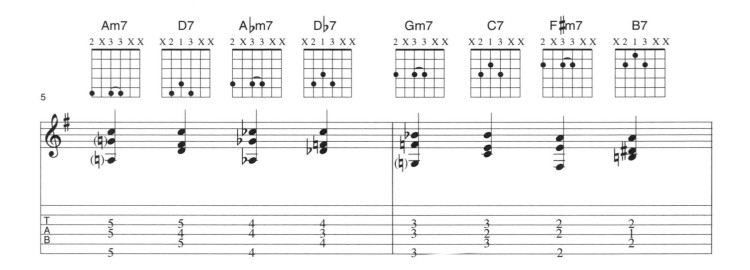

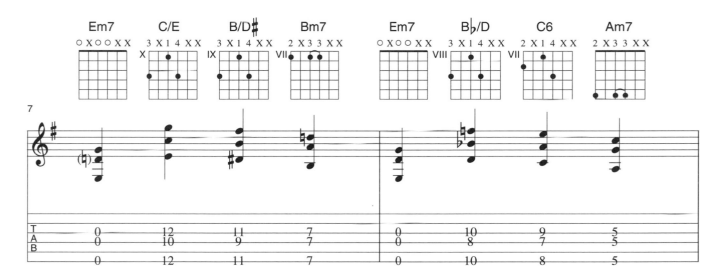

(lesson continues on next page)

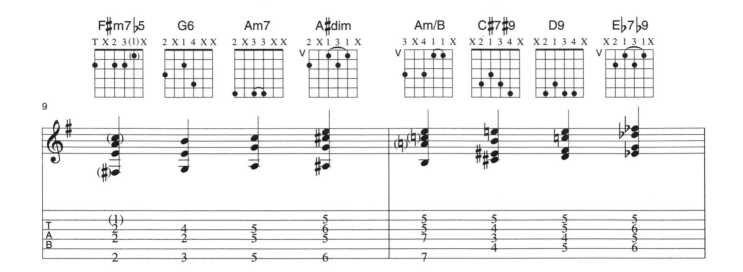

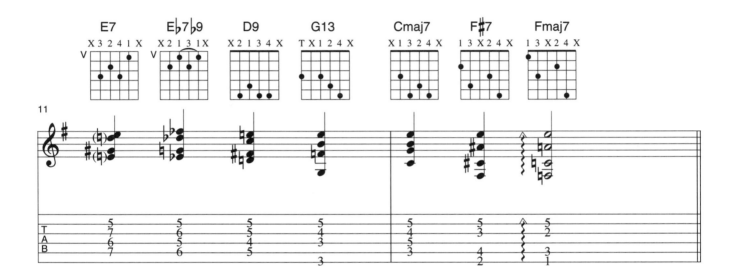

Wow, that's a lot of changes, you say. Well, on a blues like this—and it's still primarily a blues—you have to pick the spots where to go in and spell out each change, and where to just "ride" over the harmony with pentatonic ideas. I'll try to show you what works where—for instance, here's an actual playing sample of improv over the first four bars where I approach it more like the progression in Example 3.1—implying a B7, second half, bar 2, and then playing an E7♭9 idea 2nd half of bar 4. On the CD, for Examples 3.2–3.5, I play the single lines with the chords first, then follow up a second time with only the chords, so you can practice the single-line part.

Tracks
15, 16

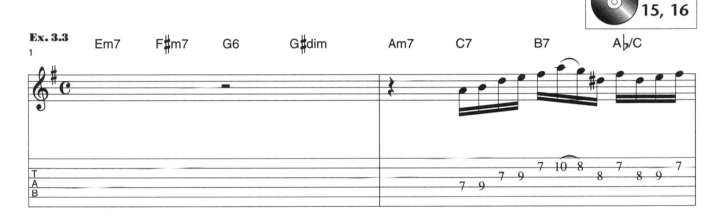

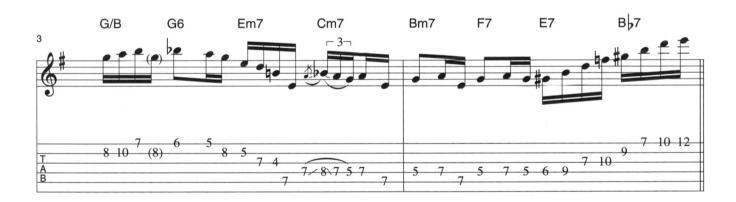

Now, for bars 5–6 (the IV section in any 12-bar blues), I suggest practicing the descending II-V7s by playing E Dorian for the Am7-D7 and continuing the same idea descending with the progression, as in Example 3.4a. For actual improvising, however, I vary the phrasing rhythmically and harmonically—see Example 3.4b. I drew from an E Superlocrian to play over the Am7-D7, and I left some holes (last 8th of bar 1, for instance) and held some notes (1st half of bar 2).

For bars 7–9 you can arpeggiate the changes (substituting relative minors for the majors—Am for C/E and G♯m for B/D♯, for instance), but you can also just play the blues—it won't clash. Example 3.5 is a trial run for bars 10–12; practice outlining the changes using the mode/scales indicated, then look at the actual lines I used.

Tracks 20, 21

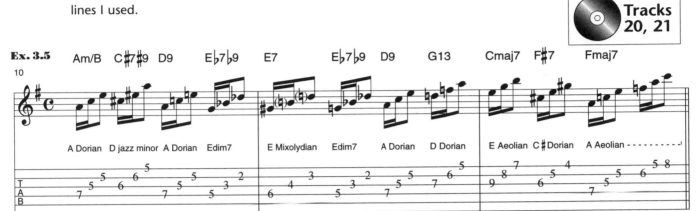

I transcribed two passes in Example 3.6 to show how it can be different each time you play, if only just slightly—both bar 11s are the same, except for the placement of a sixteenth rest in the third beat, but notice the difference in bar 10: Example 3.6a arpeggiates more, whereas Example 3.6b runs the scales. Interesting to note is how, in 3.6b, the C#7#9 and the following D9 are covered by an ascending D Dorian scale; also, in 3.6a the idea on the E♭7♭9 in bar 10 has an E natural on the end, while the same place in 3.6b has an E♭—both notes work—that's the nature of dom7♭9.

Track 22

Ex. 3.6a

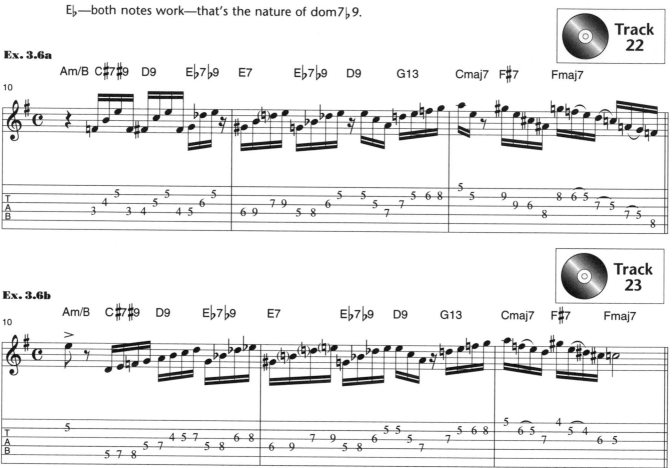

Track 23

Ex. 3.6b

OK—we've gone through the changes to "Turkish Coffee." Now
go back and try your own solo ideas on this change-laden minor
blues—you've got my support track on the CD, so take as many
passes as you like until you start getting somewhere.

Now let's look at another chord progression that uses more II-Vs.
Example 3.7 is a composition called "Arubian Nights."

Track 24

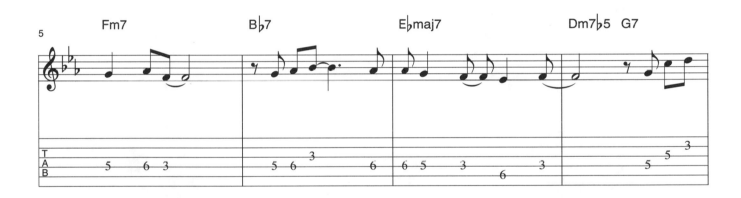

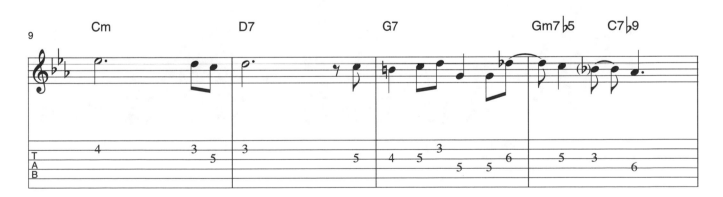

(lesson continues on next page)

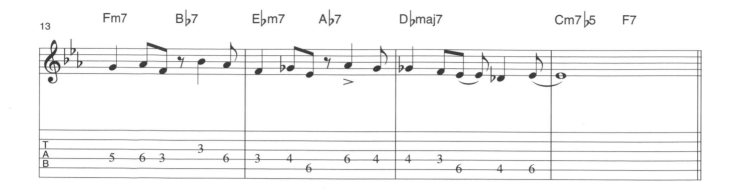

Bireli Lagrene, Richard Bona, and Billy Cobham with Larry in 1997.

Photo: Barry Morganstein

This is different from the blues progressions we've been using, with more V and II-V movement. Without going through the whole progression of "Arubian Nights," I want you to see that although this is a different song form, the same scale-rules we used playing over the blues still apply.

You don't have to play a new scale for every chord change to get into a solo, but you have to know where the tonal centers are. Looking back at the beginning of "Nights," the 1st bar tonal center is E♭ major/C minor, the 2nd bar is D7♭9, the 3rd bar tonal center is G7, and the 4th bar tonal center is C7♭9. Once you get to the Fm7 in bar 5, your tonal center is E♭. Example 3.8 is a little counterpoint-type exercise to illustrate how to go through this.

Tracks
25, 26

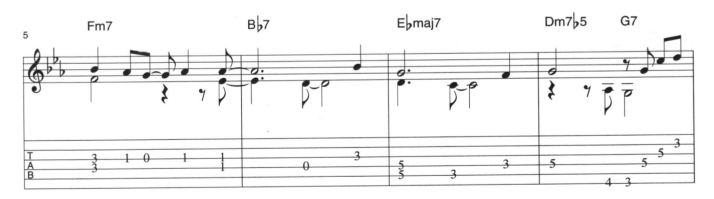

(lesson continues on next page)

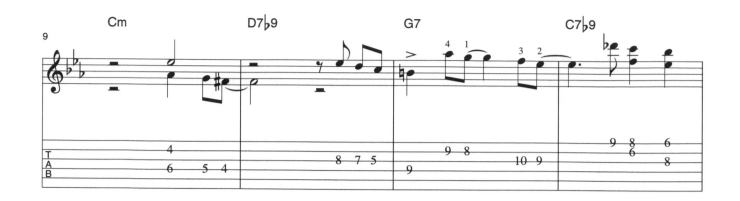

Notice the lower voice "guides" the way through the changes with harmony notes; in bar 2, the 5 of Cm (G) to the 3 of D7 (F#) and so on. The top voice is improvising, but stays close to the melody. On the CD I play the counterpoint by itself first, then a second time with the bass line.

The first time I became aware of the importance of changing scale-positions was when I was about sixteen. A "demo" player for Gibson named Andy Nelson came to our little town and played with backing tracks. He followed Johnny Smith in terms of technique, and I watched in sheer astonishment as he played ascending major-7 arpeggios at lightning speed, clean and musical.

Years later, I moved to New York and become a Gibson endorsee. I was playing with the Gary Burton Quartet at the Village Vanguard, and Andy Nelson came into the club—I guess he was still working for Gibson, because he ordered one (a cocktail, that is). Anyway, I'm indebted to Andy for his wonderful playing and for turning my attention to the great Johnny Smith, from whom I took a lesson many years later. The interesting thing is that when I asked Johnny to play those major-7 arpeggios, his fingering was different! For about thirty years, I'd been playing them "wrong." And I still am!

This is all about the role of inspiration in learning. I was inspired to emulate something that knocked me out, and in the process I developed my own fingering. As Johnny Mac once told me (when we were messing around with "Giant Steps" changes), "Fingering is everything."

So let's get into some fingering as we start to connect scale positions on the neck; we'll use a C-major scale and use C, E, and B as our starting notes. The Phrygian and Locrian scales are marked for reference only—the important thing here is shifting around the fingering to scale (pun intended) upward.

We'll start with some common C chord placements in Example 3.9; the scale variations will relate to these positions.

Ex. 3.9

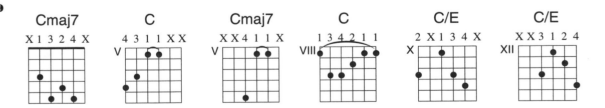

The position of a scale is determined by where the first finger is. In other words, the first Cmaj7 chord has the first finger on the third fret; but when we play the scale, the second finger goes to that same fret, fifth string, and the first finger goes to the second fret, fourth string. So this scale is played from the second postition. Example 3.10 uses the second and fifth positions, with an "option" scale route that has you jumping to the 2nd string earlier, on the D of the second octave.

Ex. 3.10

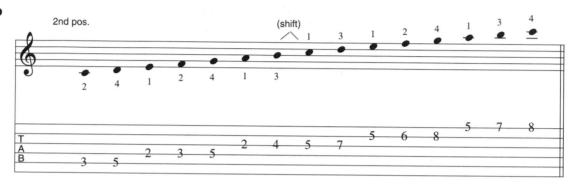

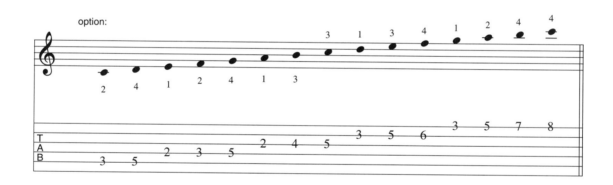

Example 3.11 starts in the 2nd position like the previous variations, but it quickly passes through several positions on its way to
high C; an alternate route is to do the first seven notes from the
fifth position (starting on the eighth fret of the sixth string). The
descent involves some downshifting and finger-shifting (marked by
an "s"). A 1-1 shift, for instance, means to move the first finger from
fret to fret.

Ex. 3.11

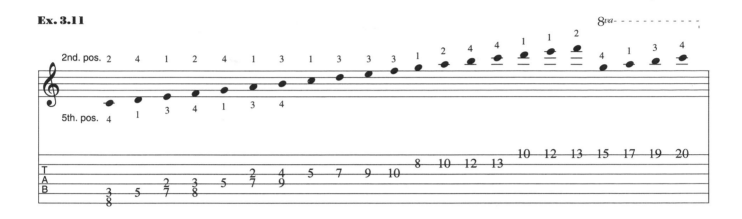

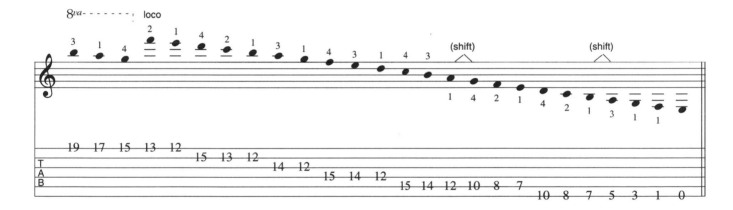

Example 3.12 takes bars 9–12 from Example 1.4 to show an
elementary example of position-shifting; the line starts with a sliding
pickup into the 5th position, goes to an "adjusted" fifth position
(like playing the first 2 chords in Example 3.9) and descends in the
third bar down the first string into the first position:

Ex. 3.12

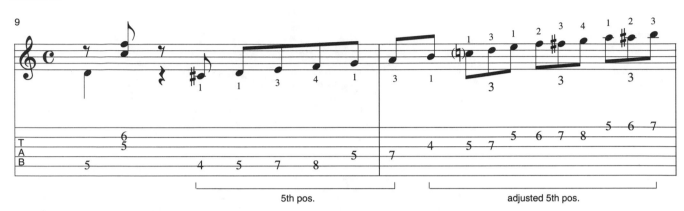

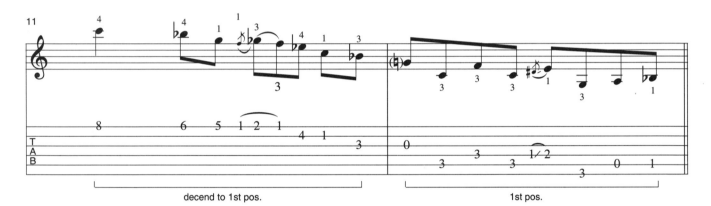

Example 3.13 starts from, first, the third degree (E), then the seventh degree (B) in the 7th and 12th positions.

Ex. 3.13

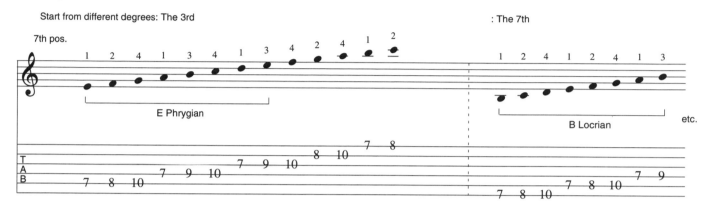

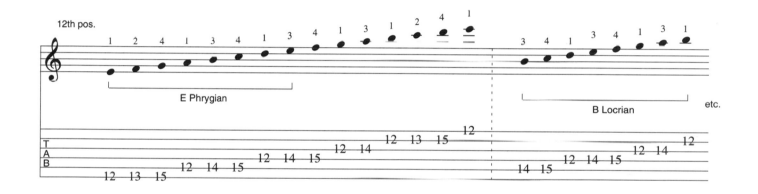

Example 3.14 goes from middle E to high A in the little-used 10th position. Notice the two whole step jumps on strings five and four; the fingering can be 1-3-4 or 1-2-4 at those points.

Ex. 3.14

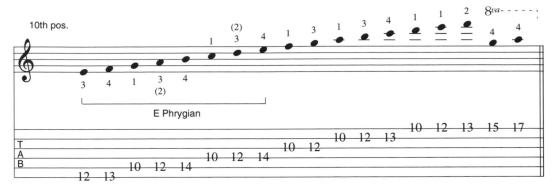

After you've looked at these positioning-fingering variations, take them into keys other than C, and play minor variations as well. You'll find you may want to make adjustments to your technique, using more "uncomfortable" jumps, successive fingering, and down-shifting to be able to connect all the various positions on the neck. Then, when you're creating ideas on the spur of the moment, you'll be better prepared to execute the needed technique. To show you what I mean, I want to go deeper into the improv tools we've looked at so far and expand the harmonic and rhythmic possibilities.

Elements of Improv

There's a sweet sadness and melancholy beauty to minor chords, so let's explore that sector of the harmonic universe. The lesson here is finding substitutions in a minor key and applying the appropriate scale/arpeggio to each chord change.

The analysis presented in this chapter may seem rather theoretical, but this is not something I decided to throw in just to disseminate information. Through the process of analysis and study, you eventually learn to respond quickly to a chord. It takes some time—in my case, it has taken a lot of time, especially to avoid the trap of shifting into "intellectual" gear in the middle of playing viscerally.

This is one of the most important ideas in improvising: You have to study the more difficult aspects of jazz in order to train yourself to altered harmonies in response-time and ear-sensitivity. Use your mind as much as possible when studying these rather gnarly topics. When it comes time to go out and play, turn your mind off and just go with the intuitive side. In other words, have fun, but the "fun" will become more musically advanced because you've broken down the difficult elements into small parts and worked out the details that would otherwise give you fits on the bandstand. This is not to say you don't use your mind *at all* when performing—you still have to know the changes, the form, etc.— but you're not in "study mode." It's a bit like extemporizing in a foreign language that you've studied and practiced.

Now to work. Play through Example 4.1 and notice that the chromatic movement of the 5 (B) up to the 6 (C♯) and back is the defining harmonic element.

(lesson continues on next page)

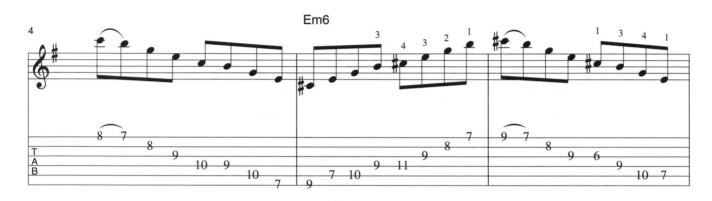

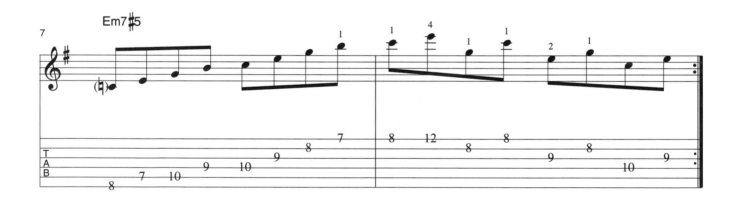

The first arpeggio starts on a B, although the tonal center is E minor; this is straight Em7, no need to think in terms of the mode. The second arpeggio is Cmaj7, and it also defines the E Aeolian mode (that's the minor mode, to refresh your memory, with the ♭7 and the ♭6). This chord could just as well be spelled as Cmaj7♯4. The Em6 uses the Locrian mode, and that arpeggio also fits in a C♯m7♭5 chord.

For a different approach to playing this progression, I constructed accompanying arpeggios in Example 4.2. You can double this with me on the CD, or solo for yourself in the open spaces. I put a simple melodic improv over one pass of the progression to give you an idea of what to do; just make sure your scales go from E minor to Cmaj♯4 to G Lydian and back to Cmaj♯4 every two bars. The mood here is "ballad" style, and I think it's a clear way to see how, as the substitutions change, so do the lines and arpeggios.

Ex. 4.2

Track 28

(lesson continues on next page)

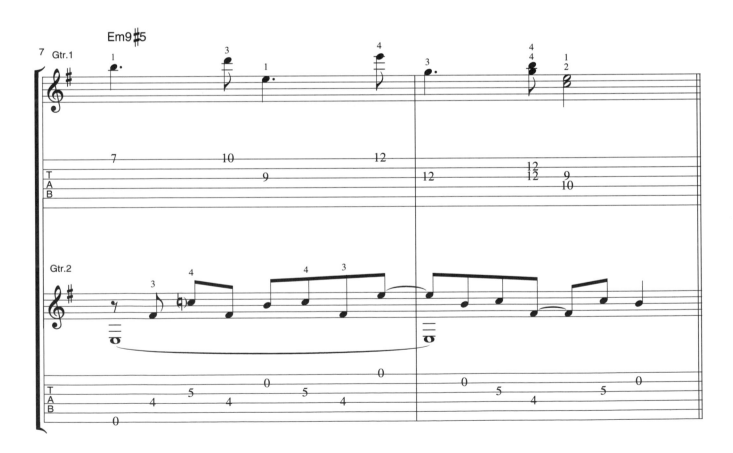

Now let's try some diminished arpeggios and phrasing that are a little more involved. Diminished exercises can be very dry, so I wrote an exercise I hope you'll find interesting. "Diminished Devil" has its own little form, a motif with variations: The first 2-bar phrase is played four times, but the second note starts a minor 3rd higher each time.

Track 29

Ex. 4.3a

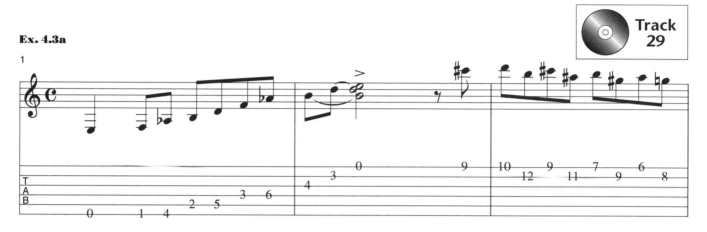

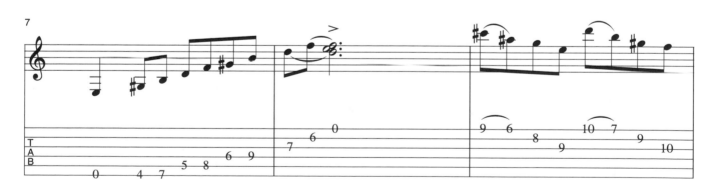

(lesson continues on next page)

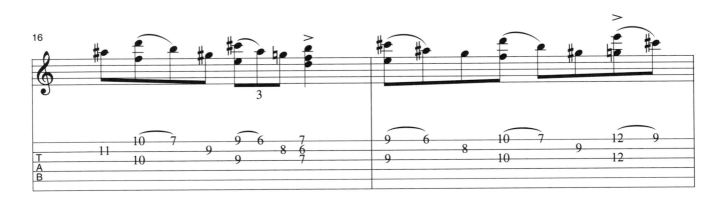

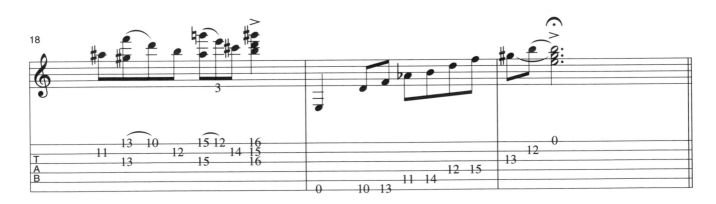

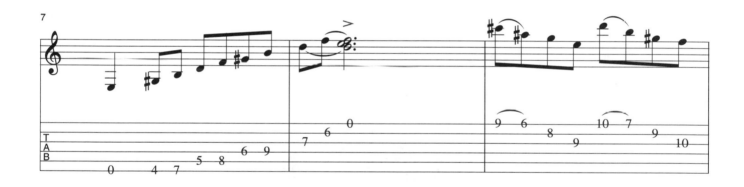

(lesson continues on next page)

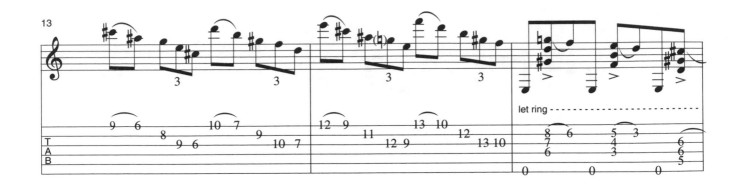

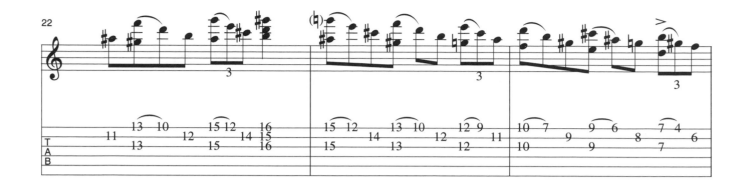

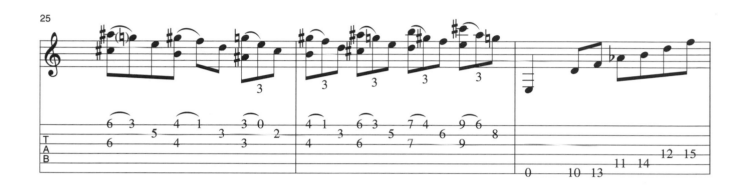

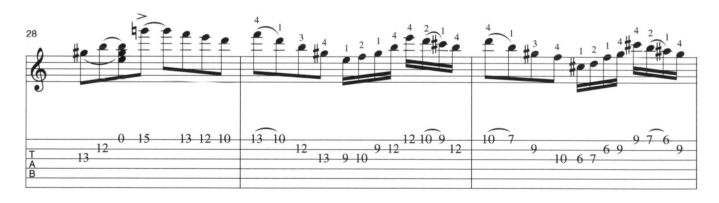

(lesson continues on next page)

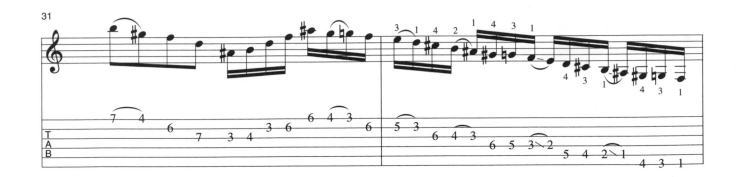

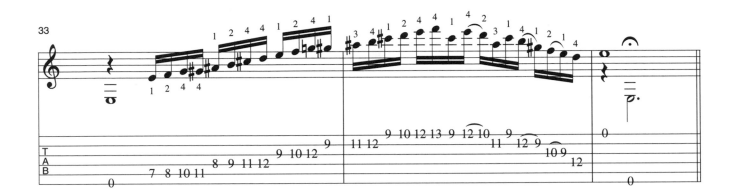

The whole thing can be thought of as playing over one long E7♭9♯9. Rhythmically, we have some 3-against-4 chords and bass note pedals going on in measures 11–12: Count one-*two*-three-one-*two*-three-one-*two* for bar 11, then one-two-*three*-one-two-*three*-rest for bar 12. For bars 15–18, know that the unaccented A♯ in the beginning of measure 16 is your downbeat—just don't accent it.

Diminished phrases can sustain interest in their own right as well as being used as passing chords and supporting dominant-7s. Listen to the CD for the timing and remember—respect those accents to liven up the phrasing.

"Diminished Devil" prepares you to go back to "Arubian Nights" (Example 3.7) and create arpeggios for each chord, using diminished arpeggios to help define the D7♭9, C7♭9, and Gm7♭5 to C7♭9. Example 4.4 is a sample over the first 12 bars. First we play the single notes only, then there's another pass with the chords. We'll do this at a slower tempo first, then bring it up to speed on the second pass.

Tracks 32, 34

Ex. 4.4

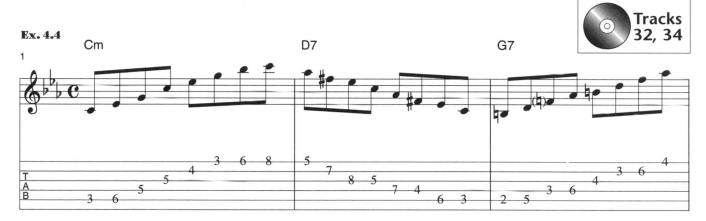

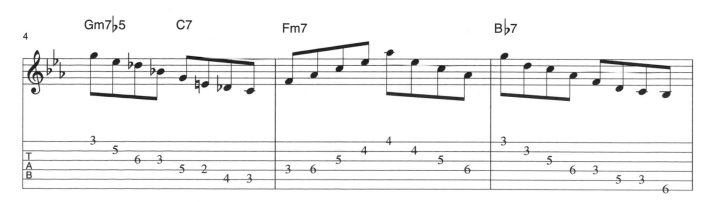

(lesson continues on next page)

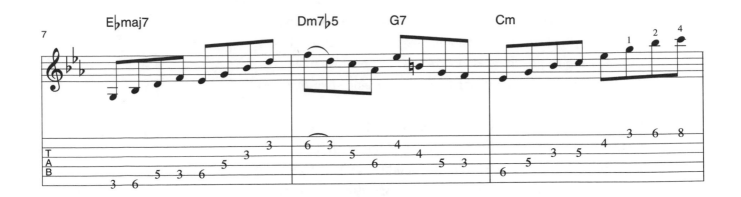

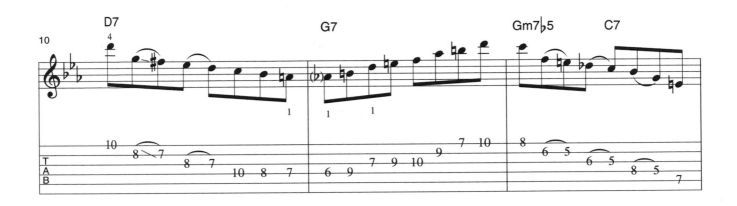

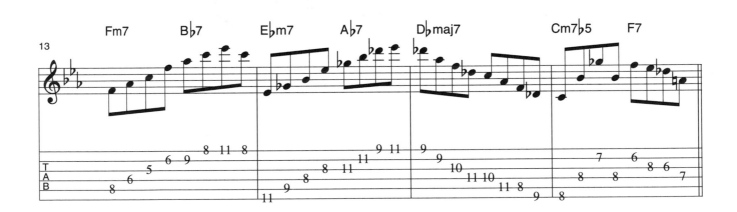

Another challenge is to create different arpeggios in the same mode in the course of negotiating substitutions. Example 4.5 shows the first four bars of "Turkish Coffee" where I've arpeggiated every change, the first three being different inversions in the E Dorian mode.

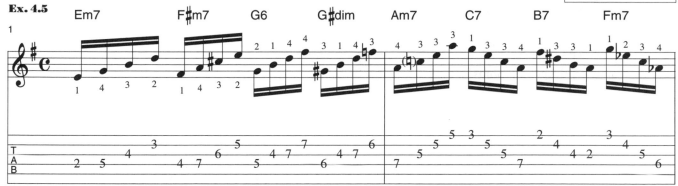

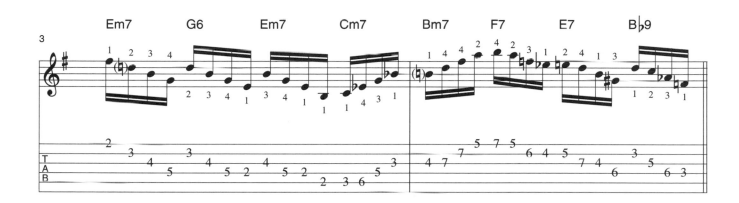

Sometimes you have to change registers when you're moving from one arpeggio to the next; the Cm7 arpeggio in the fourth beat of bar 3 leads upward, so the following Bm7 sounds more natural up an octave.

These last few exercises and examples are designed to go a little overboard as we investigate the many possibilities that can arise in the course of using a specific technique like arpeggiating. Example 4.6 is a real-world example, a recorded solo of the bridge of "Arubian Nights," that shows how I actually put arpeggios to work among single-line phrases.

Track 37

Ex. 4.6

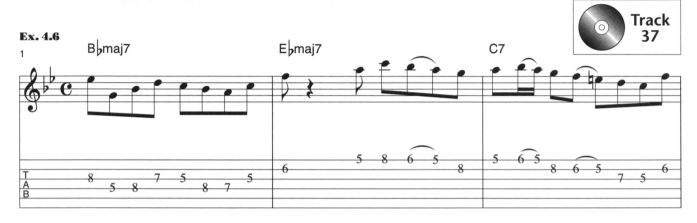

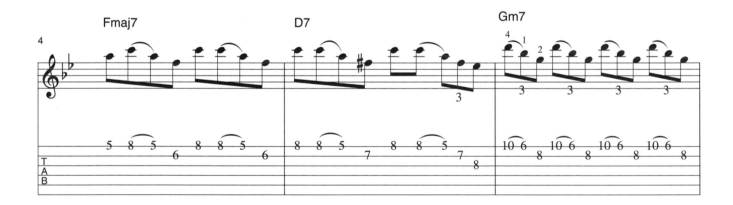

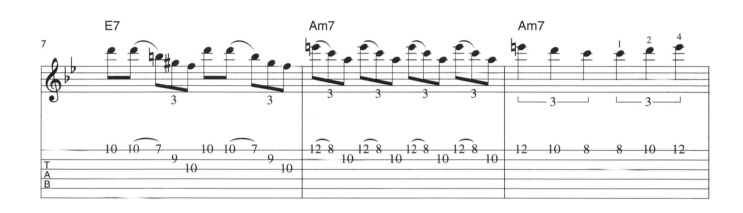

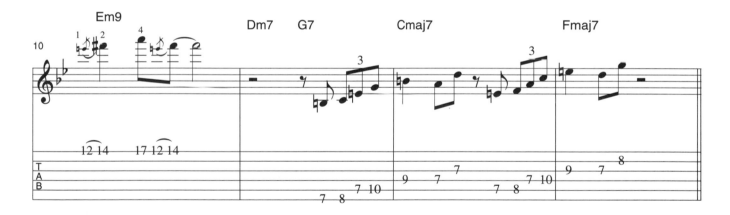

I especially like the last two phrases that are played over the Cmaj7 to Fmaj7; these arpeggios can also be used to play over Am7 to Dm7, since they're synonymous with their respective major-minor tonal centers—that is, C major with A minor and F major with D minor.

Now I want to show how there can be different harmonic con-clusions from the same or similar chords. In particular, we'll look at what I call the jazz minor scale, which is an Ionian scale with a minor 3. Let's start with 9th and m7♭5 chords and see how chang-ing them slightly can let you use an altered scale like the jazz minor.

Example 4.7 shows chord voicings (in three positions) for a C9 and an Em7♭5; then it shows the same thing for a C9♯11 and an Em7♭5/9—the same group of notes can be given either name. So you don't have to think of a different scale for a 9th chord as opposed to a m7♭5 chord—one scale will work. A C9 or Em7♭5 chord can be played with an E Locrian scale, which is the same as a B♭ Lydian scale, which is the same as F Ionian. Similarly, you can use the G jazz minor scale with a C9♯11 or Em7♭5/9 chord.

Ex. 4.7

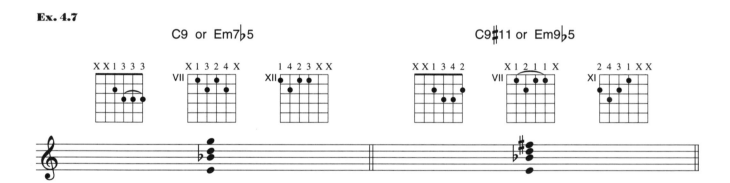

The same G jazz minor phrase can be used with a C9#11 (leading to an F13 resolution), as in Example 4.8a, or it can be used with Em7♭5/9 (leading to a G13 resolution), as in Example 4.8b. The first time includes the single line; the second time is with only the chords.

Ex. 4.8a

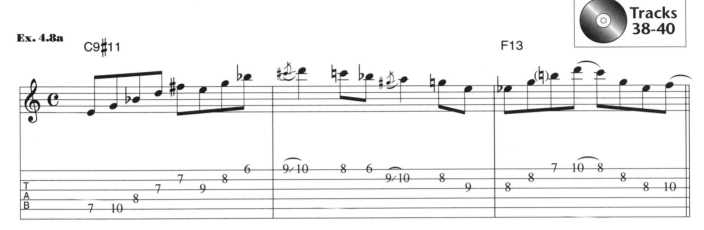

Ex. 4.8b

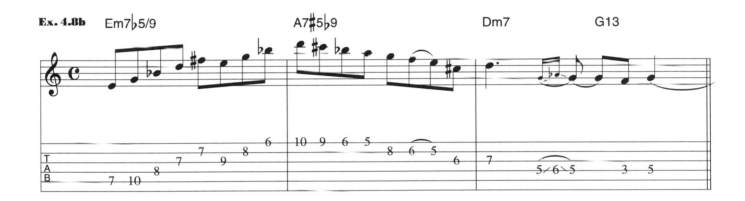

In Example 4.8a, we went to C jazz minor to cover the F13 in the third measure, while in Example 4.8b we use D harmonic minor with A as tonal center in the second measure.

Here's the same idea again: In Example 4.9a, the first phrase is a B♭ Lydian idea, two bars long, that can work with either a C9 chord or an Em7♭5 chord (or a Csus for that matter), which can lead to either an F13 or A7. Again, the first pass on the CD includes the single line; the second time is with chords only.

In Example 4.9b, we substitute F♯s for Gs, going from B♭ Lydian to the Phrygian mode of the G jazz minor scale, and, once again, this can lead to the two different resolutions, F13 or A7.

Example 4.10 arpeggiates six chords in a span of four bars, the last five using variants on the G jazz minor scale. This gives you an idea of how many ways chords out of the G jazz minor mode can be defined.

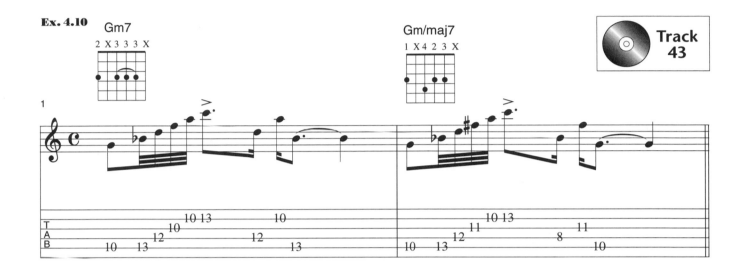

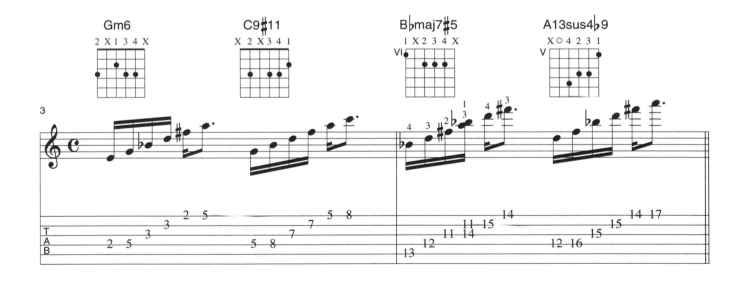

Example 4.11 uses some additional chords that call for a G jazz minor phrase, accompanied by a little line/arpeggio to define the chord. Notice how often augmented ideas pop up; there are a number of "training" features in this exercise. In bar 10, there is alternate fingering for the same phrase in bar 9. At bar 13, we use some double-stops through bar 16, leading to two voices moving (bar 18), which leads to a "composed" final four bars still using only the notes from the G jazz minor scale. Play the last note, the E harmonic on the twelfth fret, sixth string, with your right hand, while continuing to sustain the final B♭Maj7♯5 chord.

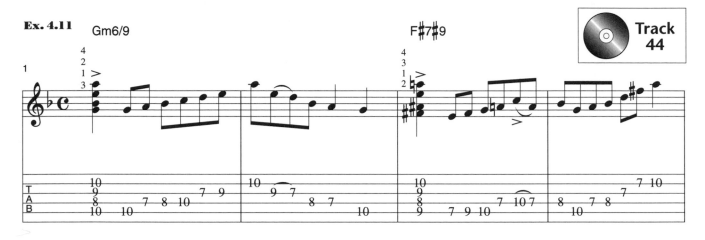

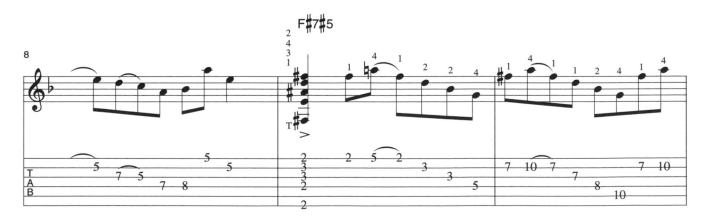

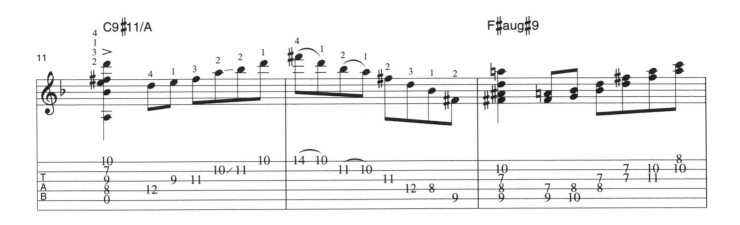

C9#11/A   F#aug#9

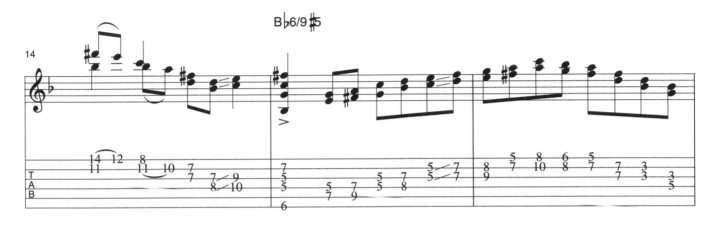

Bb6/9#5

Gm/maj7

* Hammer without picking

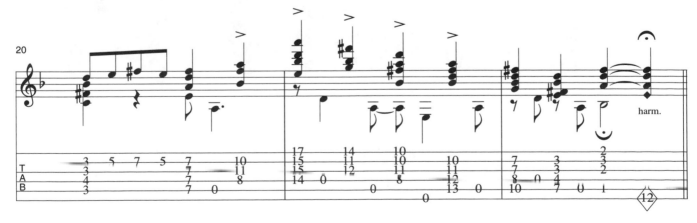

harm.

Photo: Bob Berg

Playing and Listening

You may wonder how a guitarist can develop a musical understanding of another instrument like a trumpet or saxophone. Well, I don't know exactly how it's supposed to happen, but in my early days I hung with the horn players in town and tried to absorb how they approached playing. When I'd comp for a trumpet player, the only single-note stuff I played was when I'd double be-bop heads with the horn. I concentrated on providing the harmony and rhythm, and when I'd play something that threw the horn player, he'd let me hear about it. So I learned that I really had to develop sensitivity and consideration as part of my evolution as a supporting player. I got respect from players who were more advanced than me because they could see I really wanted to learn. Later on, I started to dig the nth-degree guitar/sax combinations like Gabor Szabo with Charles Lloyd, and Jim Hall with Paul Desmond. Those collaborations paved the way for later hookups I would have with Steve Marcus and, more recently, Donald Harrison.

The basic "rules" for comping:

1. Don't step on the soloist by making your comp too busy.
2. Use space—the rhythmic choices should be off the beat and between the beats. You don't want to begin each measure by coming down on the *one*—it's too obvious and square.
3. Stay out of the soloist's register; play below (in pitch) or above. There will inevitably be some clashes, but keep them to a minimum (and sometimes they turn out OK—nice accidents happen all the time in improvised music).
4. When the soloist is playing the melody, don't double the melody notes unless it's part of an arrangement. Stick to your part and let a soloist do his or her thing.
5. Choosing how many notes are in the chords is important—sometimes two- or three-note chords are appropriate, other times you need more notes, or more open-voiced chords, or upper- or lower-voiced chords.

To show these rules in action, let's work with a bossa-nova, "Old City, New City," a straight, no-frills samba with lots of good chords. I wrote it for a Brazilian project in the early '90s called "Live from Bahia." Example 5.1 shows the first 12 bars.

Track 45

As you can see, the tune is not linear—it's arpeggiated all over the place. Nevertheless, if you're a second guitarist supporting the piece, you can do a simple Brazilian pattern of anticipatory punched chords that work underneath the written line and avoid doubling any of the melody, as in Example 5.2. On the CD, the first comp is alone; the second time, the comp is with the melody.

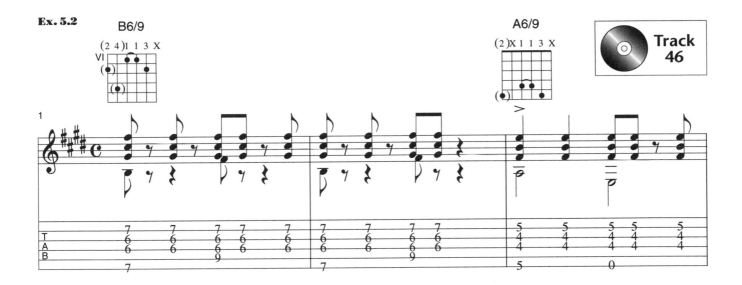

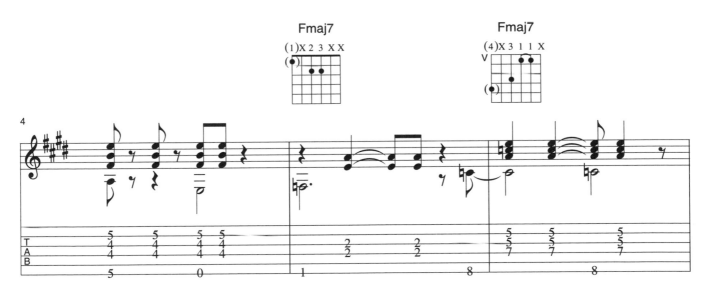

(lesson continues on next page)

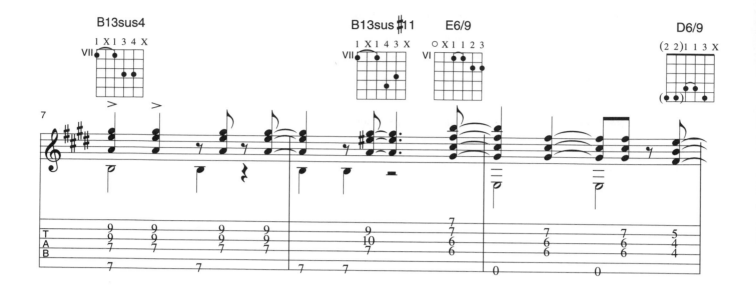

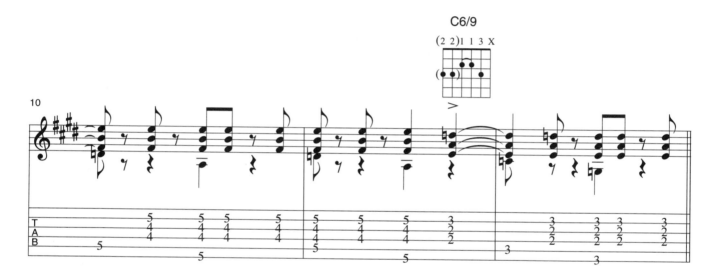

The bass notes generally come down on one and three all the way through, with the exception of bar 8, where the bass adjusts to the melody at that point. Now let's put in a solo and pretend we're playing in a small group situation.

Notice how the approach changes drastically in Example 5.3. The comping guitar uses more space, holds chords longer, and then changes things up with some rhythmic hits, as in bars 7–8, adjusting to that little jog in the melody. Again, the idea is to keep it simple and supportive for the soloist.

Ex. 5.3

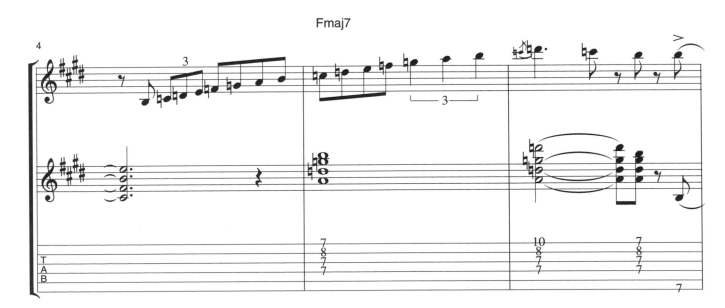

(lesson continues on next page)

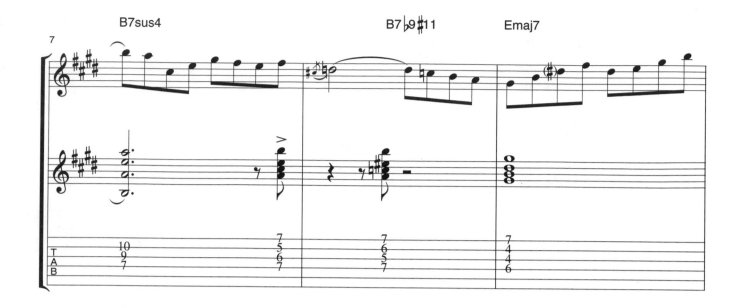

Next, I want to show you a real-life example from a concert featuring altoist Donald Harrison on a tune of mine called "Dragon Gate." Example 5.4 shows how my comping relates to the alto solo: It stays underneath, keeps some open spaces, and, when appropriate, offers a little reply or echo to what the horn is doing.

Track 49

Ex. 5.4

* Alto sax solo notated in concert pitch.

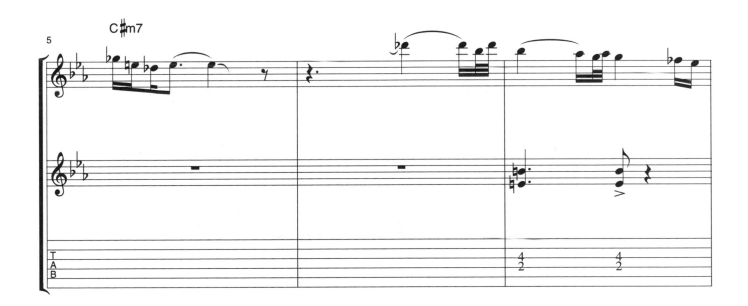

(lesson continues on next page)

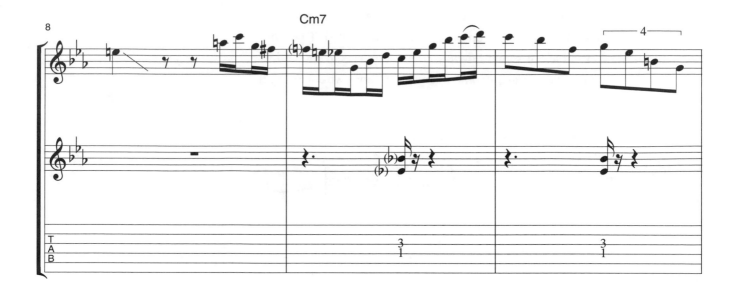

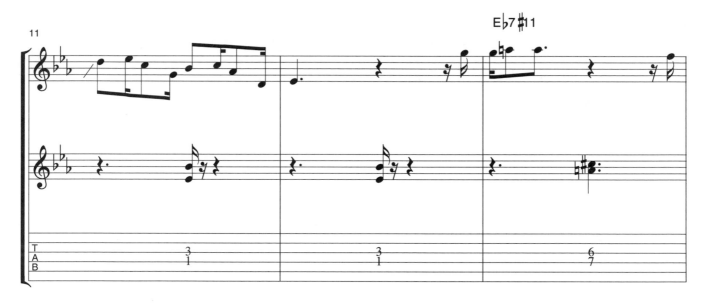

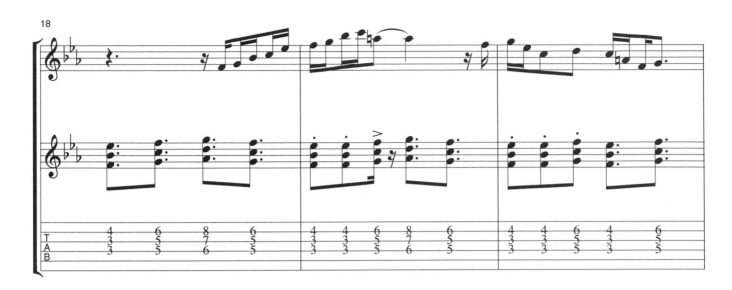

C#m7

Cm7

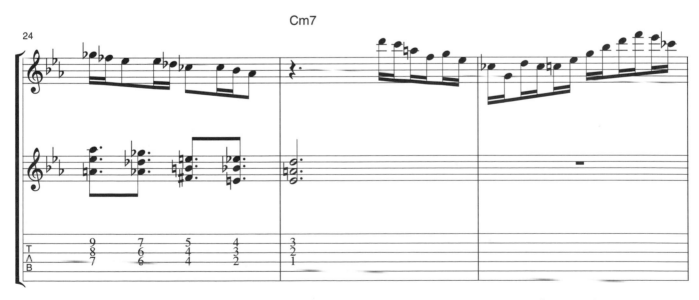

(lesson continues on next page)

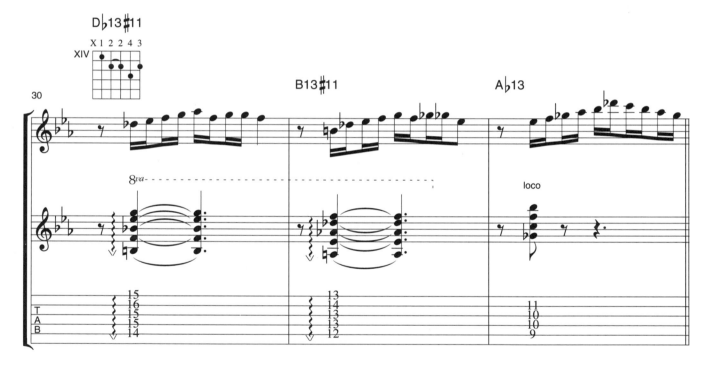

The guitar answers the horn in bars 13–17; notice the guitar is quiet when the horn is busy. In the second chorus (starting at bar 17), the guitar avoids playing on the downbeat—important. The horn is blowing in one rhythmic pattern while the guitar does its own pattern underneath, based on a four-against-six polyrhythm (see Example 5.5).

Ex. 5.5

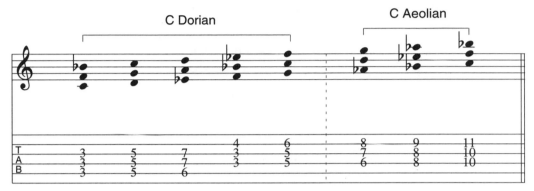

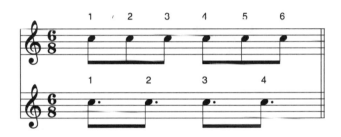

The chords follow a chord-scale where the first five steps are
C Dorian and the final three steps are C Aeolian. Now, because I
don't want to infringe on the soloist's register, I hardly ever use the
final two chords of the scale, stopping instead at the ♭VI. It turns
out that the ♭VI chord form, an Fm6 without the root but an Fm6
nevertheless, becomes a substitute for the Im (Cm). Of course, this
applies only to the Cm portion of "The Dragon Gate" progression;
the Dorian-Aeolian chord-scale moves up a half-step when we go
to the C♯m.

The guitar lays out in bars 26–29; the rhythm section is churning
behind the horn. When the guitar enters, it's on beat 2, not the
downbeat. Those D♭13♯11 and B13♯11 chords in 30–31 may not be
known to you, but grab on to that voicing—it's very effective.
Notice the root is not played; the bass takes care of that.

The chord sequence from the four-against-six has an additional
use in the out-vamp of the piece; this section also shows how the
soloist (alto sax) and comper (guitar) can switch roles; the horn
repeats the vamp figure while the guitar plays a free-floating single
line (first four bars of Example 5.6) followed by eight bars of the
minor-scale chords from bars 17–25 in Example 5.4. In the out-vamp,
however, there's no Fm chord substituted after the V interval; it's a
straight Cm6/9 played on strings five through two.

Ex. 5.6

Track 51

* Alto sax solo notated in concert pitch.

So the guitar is actually carrying the ball melodically here while the alto provides an ostinato support. It's not a solo per se, since the dynamic level of both instruments is *mp*; it's a form of interplay.

There's another form of interplay that can arise in the horn/guitar combination. The guitar can start out in its traditional role of staccato chord support and then ease up into the horn's register (rules are made to be broken, and here's an example) and the two can hit some phrases together spontaneously. These accidents of togetherness occur because both players are interpreting the rhythm the same way.

Example 5.7 is a fragment of an opus called "Good Citizen Swallow," which has several between-the-beat accents in the melody.

Ex. 5.7

Each chorus is fifteen bars long. When you throw in those push-
ing accents in an odd-numbered bar form, you can get choruses like
Example 5.8.

Ex. 5.8

Track
53

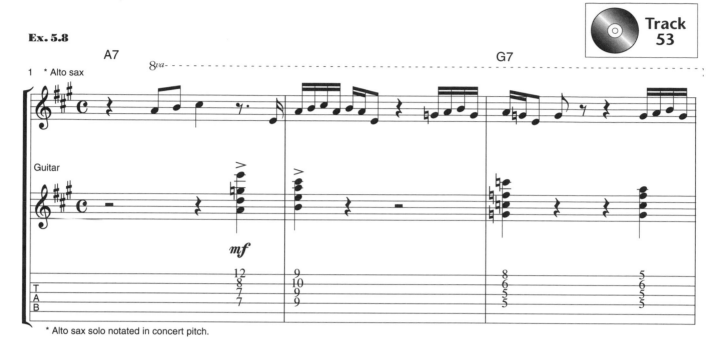

* Alto sax solo notated in concert pitch.

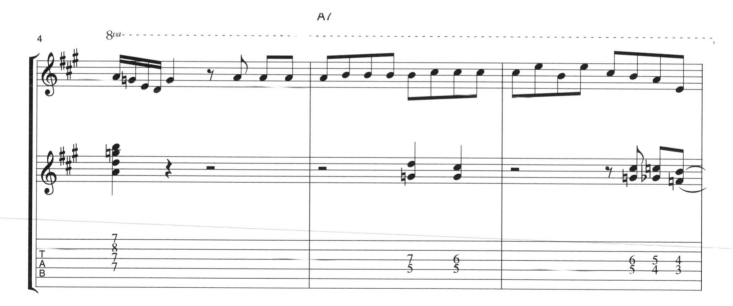

(lesson continues on next page)

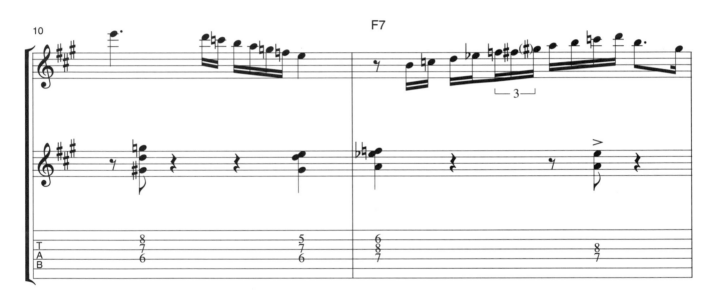

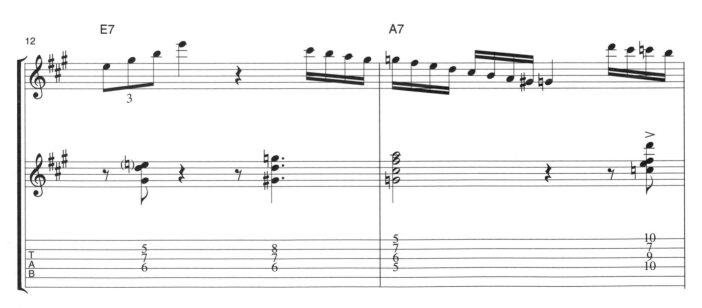

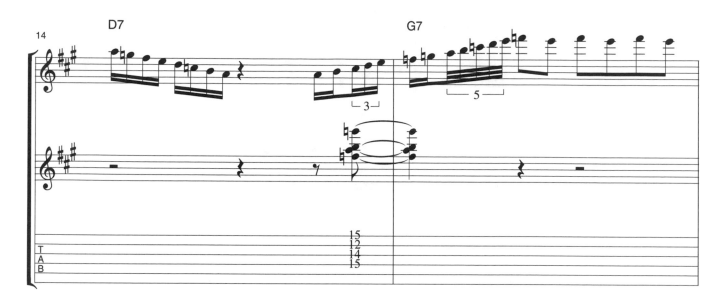

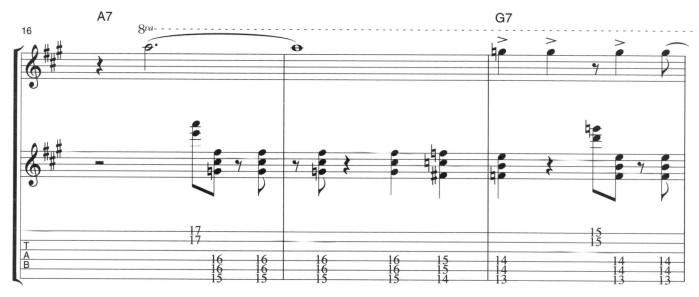

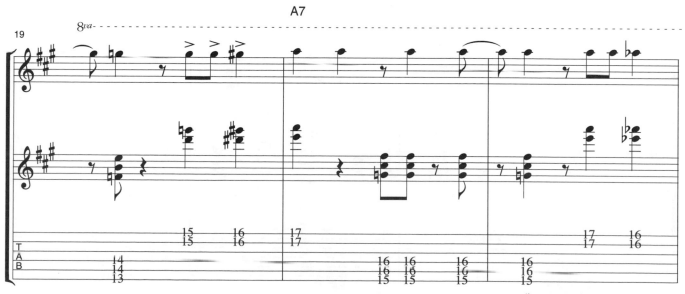

(lesson continues on next page)

Note that when the alto is playing a lot of notes in the first chorus, especially bars 9–15, the comping guitar really has to be sparse. Notice also that at the beginning of the second chorus (bar 16) the guitar has moved from the middle part of the neck to around the 10th fret; at that point, the nucleus of the A13 and G13 chords is fingered on strings six, five, and four, and the left hand pinky covers the 4ths on strings two and one. Even at the climax of the interplay between alto and guitar, the guitar still avoids coming down on the *one* (look at bar 16—half-measure rest before hitting that three and chord hit). The comper—that's me—does come down on the one in this section (1st beat, bar 18, for example) but a lot of that is because I'm phrasing together with the horn; once that little spontaneous unison section subsides, the guitar goes back to its supporting role (bar 25) and plays some of the same comp-phrases as before (look at the similarity between bars 27–28 and bars 12–13).

FINAL WORD

Let's pull back from the details of comping for an overview of what we've been doing: We've looked at the blues and some necessary theoretical principles and devices to learn a musical language and communicate in that language. We've worked with specific scales and chords and chord scales as well as exercises to develop playing; many more exercises and lessons are out there. Look at them and see how they relate to what you've learned in this book—it's an ever expanding quest. We've also taken certain song forms and broken them down for analysis to develop subtle ways to improvise. You'll be able to recognize the basic ideas that run through most progressions, so you can tackle most any tune or composition.

Now you should be solidly grounded in the fundamentals of what it takes to play jazz. I encourage you to go out and play with some other musicians and test yourself; when you play with musicians who are more experienced than you, be sure to ask questions. You never stop learning. Keep this seeking spirit with you. This music we play is rich in choices and nuances; you never (at least in my opinion) will arrive at the ultimate plateau and say, "I don't need to learn more."

As a bassist told me years ago, "In jazz you have to play the percentages." This means that you're allowed to always try for that "perfect" solo or "perfect" performance. But in all likelihood you're not going to get it—just a piece of it. The reward comes in trying—going for it. So I'll close now by saying to you: go for it—do your best—and remember that no effort in pursuit of quality playing is ever wasted. All the best...peace.

Photo: Caspari De Geus

One of the pioneers of jazz-rock, Larry Coryell's eclectic musical career began when he was a teenager playing in a band led by pianist Mike Mandel. By 1965 he replaced Gabor Szabo in Chico Hamilton's band. In 1966, he debuted on Hamilton's *The Dealer* album and played with a proto-jazz-rock band, the Free Spirits. In 1967-68 Coryell played with Gary Burton's combo, and was one of the most prominent solo voices on Herbie Mann's popular *Memphis Underground* album (recorded in 1968). He, Mandel and Steve Marcus formed a group called Foreplay in 1969 (no relation to today's Fourplay), which by 1973 had become the core of the jazz-rock band Eleventh House.

In 1975, Coryell, concentrating on acoustic guitar, produced a series of duo and trio sessions with Philip Catherine, Emily Remler, John Scofield, Joe Beck, Steve Khan and John McLaughlin. In the mid-'80s, Coryell toured with McLaughlin and Paco DeLucia, and in 1986 participated in a five-way guitar session with Tal Farlow, Scofield, Larry Carlton and John Abercrombie for the Jazzvisions series. Coryell has also recorded with Stephane Grappelli, Charles Mingus, Sonny Rollins and Kenny Barron, and has taped Brazilian music with Dori Caymmi for CTI, mainstream jazz for Muse, solo guitar for Shanachie, and (for Nippon Phonogram in Japan) an album of classical transcriptions of music by Stravinsky and Rimsky-Korsakov.

—Excerpted from the *All Music Guide to Jazz, 3rd Edition*

When it Comes to Music We Wrote the Book

Guitar Player Sessions
Licks & Lessons from the World's Greatest Guitar Players and Teachers

Edited by Andy Ellis
These guitar lessons in rock, blues, jazz, country, and more reflect the provocative mix any serious guitarist wants: masterful tips and tricks for the next gig, plus creative ideas for brighter musical style. Companion audio CD lets players hear key lessons from the book—note for note.
Softcover with audio CD, 80pp, 8-1/2 x 11, ISBN 0-87930-503-7, $17.95

Hot Guitar
Rock Soloing, Blues Power, Rapid-Fire Rockabilly, Slick Turnarounds, and Cool Licks

By Arlen Roth
This collection of hot techniques and cool licks includes detailed instruction and hundreds of musical examples. Drawing on ten years of the "Hot Guitar" column from *Guitar Player*, this book covers string bending, slides, picking and fingering techniques, soloing, and rock, blues, and country licks.
Softcover, 160pp, 8-1/2 x 11, ISBN 0-87930-276-3, $19.95

The Player's Guide to Guitar Maintenance

By Dave Burrluck
This helpful book with step-by-step photographs shows exactly how to adjust an electric guitar so it is perfectly matched with your own playing style. Focusing on non-technical adjustments and straight forward advice, this book covers such topics as adjusting strings, necks, vibratos, and the cleaning and care of your instrument.
Hardcover, 84 pp, 200 color photos, 8-1/2 x 11, ISBN 0-87930-549-5, $24.95

Do-It-Yourself Projects for Guitarists
35 Useful, Inexpensive Electronic Projects to Help Unlock Your Instrument's Potential

By Craig Anderton
A step-by-step guide for electric guitarists who want to create maximum personalized sound with minimum electronic problems, and get the satisfaction of achieving all this themselves.
Softcover, 171pp, 100 line drawings, 7-3/8 x 10-7/8, ISBN 0-87930-359-X, $19.95

Guitar Player Repair Guide
How to Set Up, Maintain, and Repair Electrics and Acoustics— Second Edition

By Dan Erlewine
Whether you're a player, collector, or repairperson, this hands-on guide provides all the essential information on caring for guitars and electric basses. With hundreds of photos and drawings, this revised edition includes new tools, techniques, and detailed specs on specific models.
Softcover, 309pp, 250 illustrations, 8-1/2 x 11, ISBN 0-87930-291-7, $22.95

All Music Guide to Jazz
The Experts' Guide to the Best Jazz Recordings—3rd Edition

Edited by Michael Erlewine, Vladimir Bogdanov, Chris Woodstra, and Scott Yanow

"This is simply the best single-volume jazz reference book available."
—American Reference Books Annual

Now a classic for jazz lovers and newcomers alike, this easy-to-use guide reviews and rates more than 14,000 sizzling recordings by over 1,500 artists in everything from New Orleans jazz to bebop and beyond.
Softcover, 1,400pp, 50 charts, 7-3/8 x 9-1/4, ISBN 0-87930-530-4, $29.95

Singing Jazz
The Singers and Their Styles

By Bruce Crowther and Mike Pinfold
This is the story of the jazz singer's vibrant world, where the voice itself is an instrument and the art of improvisation and self-expression reigns. This book explores the fascinating lives and diverse music of dozens of jazz vocalists past and present—from Louis Armstrong to Kitty Margolis—offering insightful inspiration for young jazz singers and an entertaining backstage tour for jazz lovers.
Softcover, 288pp, 57 B&W photos, 6-1/8 x 9-1/4, ISBN 0-87930-519-3, $17.95

Jaco
The Extraordinary and Tragic Life of Jaco Pastorius, "The World's Greatest Bass Player"

By Bill Milkowski
This is a fitting tribute to the talented but tormented genius who revolutionized the electric bass and single-handedly fused jazz, classical, R&B, rock, reggae, pop, and punk—all before the age of 35, when he met his tragic death.
Softcover with CD, 264pp, 6 x 9, ISBN 0-87930-426-X, $14.95

The Hammond Organ
Beauty in the B

By Mark Vail
This book salutes the instrumental pairing that has changed the sound of the organ in gospel, blues, jazz, R&B, rock, and pop since the 1950s: the Hammond B-3 and the whirling Leslie speaker. This loving history describes the mechanical innovations and musical influence of this legendary pairing.
Softcover, 239pp, 29 color photos, 240 B&W photos, 8-1/2 x 11, ISBN 0-87930-459-6, $24.95

The Sax & Brass Book
Saxophones, Trumpets and Trombones in Jazz, Rock and Pop

Edited by Tony Bacon
This is the first illustrated history of the horns that have defined jazz and enhanced rock, pop, and R&B with an astonishingly expressive range of distinctive, classy sounds. A bright mix of sparkling color photography and engaging narrative, the book explores the evolving music, brilliant musicians, and leading makers of these inspiring instruments from the 1920s to 1990s.
Hardcover, 112pp, 200 color photos, 7-1/2 x 9-3/4, ISBN 0-87930-531-2, $24.95

What's on the CD

Track 1—Tune-Up

Track 2—Example 1.1

Track 3—Example 1.4

Track 4—Example 1.5

Track 5—Example 1.6

Track 6—Example 1.7

Track 7—Example 2.2

Track 8—Example 2.2 plus 1.1

Track 9—Example 2.3

Track 10—Example 2.4a

Track 11—Example 2.4b

Track 12—Example 2.5

Track 13—Example 2.6

Track 14—Example 3.2

Track 15—Example 3.3

Track 16—Basic Track of 3.3

Track 17—Example 3.4a

Track 18—Example 3.4b

Track 19—Chords from Track 18

Track 20—Example 3.5

Track 21—Chords from Track 20

Track 22—Example 3.6a

Track 23—Example 3.6b

Track 24—Example 3.7

Track 25—Example 3.8

Track 26—Track 25 with Bass Line

Track 27—Example 4.1

Track 28—Example 4.2

Track 29—Example 4.3a Slow,
        then Fast

Track 30—"Diminished Devil"
        Explanation

Track 31—Example 4.3b, Slow,
        then Fast

Track 32—Example 4.4

Track 33—Example 4.4 with Chords

Track 34—Track 33, Faster

Track 35—Larry Talks About 4.5

Track 36—Example 4.5

Track 37—Example 4.6

Track 38—Larry Talks About 4.8

Track 39—Examples 4.8a and 4.8b

Track 40—Chords for Track 39

Track 41—Examples 4.9a and 4.9b

Track 42—Chords for Track 41

Track 43—Example 4.10

Track 44—Example 4.11

Track 45—Example 5.1

Track 46—Example 5.2

Track 47—Examples 5.1 and 5.2

Track 48—Example 5.3

Track 49—Example 5.4

Track 50—Example 5.5

Track 51—Example 5.6

Track 52—Example 5.7

Track 53—Example 5.8

Ken Rich, CD Engineer

All compositions and exercises composed by Larry Coryell, Coryell Publishing/Deganawidah Music/BMI

Tracks 49, 51, 53: Recorded live on the Ford/AirTouch Cellular Stage at the 1997 Ford Montreux Detroit Jazz Festival on August 31, 1997. Recording produced by WEMU, Ypsilanti, public radio at Eastern Michigan University. Executive Director: Art Timko; Producer: Michael Jewett; Live stereo recording by Paul Townsend, Assisted by Harold Beer. Stage sound by Aerial Enterprises. The Ford Montreux Detroit Jazz Festival is produced by Music Hall Center for the Performing Arts.

Kenwood Dennard, Drums

Bill Foster, Bass

Donald Harrison, Alto